In *The Apple of His Eye*, a moving sequel to Miriam Finesilver's *Naomi, the Rabbi's Wife*, we follow Naomi and Daniel as they face the many challenges to their identity as Jews and followers of Yeshua (Jesus). Along the way, we meet their daughter Tamara, who is bright and creative, yet conflicted, and her Yiddishe bubbe (grandmother) Helen, and an assortment of other engaging characters. This book will keep you rapt and engaged to the tender and touching conclusion.

Rabbi Michael Robert Wolf
Author of *The Upper Zoo, The Linotype Operator,* and
The Linotype Legacy

As a sequel to Miriam Finesilver's *Naomi the Rabbi's Wife*, the story of Daniel and Naomi picks up right where her first book left off—will Daniel move forward with having been confronted with the truth that Yeshua is the true Messiah of the Jewish people? Although this is a sequel, have no fear! You will walk right into the reality of Temple Beth Shalom and Daniel and Naomi's home in Boca Raton, and move right along with the continuing story of this loving couple—oh, and not to mention this is a trilogy in the offing—therefore, *Apple of His Eye* will leave you awaiting the third of this series.

You will find Mrs. Finesilver does a masterful job of writing dialogue and making the reader feel the emotions of a husband and wife, deeply in love, in their joys and in their disagreements.

Nancy Petrey
Author of *Jewish Roots Journey, Family Secrets - Divine Destinies,*
and *Why Christians Should Care about Their Jewish Roots.*

The dialogue is masterfully written. I feel I can actually "hear" the characters speaking. It's like watching a movie. The characters have such depth and range. They feel alive to me.

The pace is fast-moving, with lots of twists, turns and surprises. Anything but boring! Every page comes alive. No tedium ever with this author.

This was one of the rare sequels that did not require me to read the first of the series to understand and enjoy it. Start here, and then go back to the first book. It will be a wonderful prequel to this captivating – and meaningful – story.

Elizabeth Brickman, Author
THIN & BLESSED

The Apple of His Eye

Miriam Finesilver

Energion Publications
Gonzalez, Florida
2022

Though they may resemble groups that you know, all persons, groups, and events mentioned in this book are fictional, created for dramatic effect.

Center front cover image by Hannah May, painted for this book.

ISBN: 978-1-63199-812-6
eISBN: 978-1-63199-813-3

Energion Publications
P. O. Box 841
Gonzalez, Florida 32560

energion.com
pubs@energion.com

Table of Contents

DEDICATION

James 1:17: "Every good gift and every perfect gift is from above, and cometh down from the Father of lights, with whom is no variableness, neither shadow of turning."

Thank you, Abba, for the most precious gifts You have given me:

Michael, after I prayed James 1:17, Abba Father gave me the gift that still leaves me breathless. I can't imagine life without you, Michael—and I don't want to!

Another gift was given to me years and years before I knew to appreciate her. Mom, if only I knew how beautiful you were when you were here, but you are now with Yeshua and experiencing love beyond measure.

Temple
Beth Shalom

6400 Mizner Court
Boca Raton, FL 33432

June 21, 1988

United Synagogue for Conservative Judaism
120 Broadway, Suite 1540
New York NY 20271

Attention: Joint Placement Commission

Dear Sirs and Madams:
We write to you with a heavy heart stating our urgent need for either a permanent or interim rabbi.
We at Temple Beth Shalom are grief-stricken. Perhaps by now you have learned of the grievous scandal
concerning Daniel Cantor (may his name be blotted out). This blasphemer had been our rabbi
for the last five years.

We excused his youth and were actually pleasantly surprised as he brought in the younger generation
who have since joined our membership roster. However, two weeks ago, upon returning from a
congregational trip to Israel, Mr. Cantor resigned as our rabbi. He did so after announcing his
conversion to Christianity.

His wife was always a bit unusual and we have determined it was her influence that corrupted our
once-beloved rabbi. As you can imagine, this has brought confusion to our synagogue and we fear
our membership will rapidly decline.

Please help us with this urgent need for pulpit supply. I, along with our Search Committee, will
gladly fly to New York to meet with you in person if this would help expedite this situation.

Sincerely,

Jay Marcus

President, Temple Beth Shalom

**Associated
Synagogues
of Conservative
Judaism**

120 Broadway, Suite 1540 New York NY 20271

June 28, 1988

Temple Beth Shalom
6400 Mizner Court
Boca Raton, FL 33432

Attn: Jay Marcus, President

Dear Mr. Marcus:

We mourn with you and the members of your congregation and have alerted Rabbi Moskowitz about your unfortunate situation as he was your rabbi before Daniel Cantor. Rabbi Moskowitz is heartbroken hearing this news and he and his wife are quickly making arrangements to travel to Boca Raton. He has agreed to serve as interim rabbi while we begin a search for proper candidates for your congregation.

Rabbi Moskowitz will be contacting you shortly—or perhaps even as we write this, you have already heard from him.

Sincerely,

Sarah Kaplan

Chair Joint Placement Committee

Chapter One

Two Weeks Earlier

"Let us welcome the *Shabbat* together. Psalm 95 in your *Siddur*, please," Daniel instructed the congregation in his soft yet authoritative voice.

Sitting in the first row, her hands shaking, Naomi followed her husband's instructions and reached for her prayer book. Oh no! The hiccups began. This used to happen all the time when she was nervous, but it had been a long time since an attack. And it must have been audible enough for Renee, sitting on the same bench, to scooch over and gently tap Naomi's back. It didn't help. Daniel gave her a sidelong glance, which Naomi met with a faint smile—just as another hiccup convulsed her body.

A few deep breaths halted the attack and she could now hear the familiar sound of pages being turned. This familiar sound would be the last familiar anything for this evening. Maybe for the rest of her life. To the members of the Temple it was just another *Shabbat* service. But she and Daniel knew they were venturing into uncharted territories.

"Preserve me, dear Lord, for in You I put my trust. The verses Naomi had memorized from Psalm 16 months and months ago, silenced all other sounds around her. *Oh my soul, you have said unto the Lord, you are my God. You are the portion of my inheritance, and you have maintained my lot. I have set You before me, because You are at my right hand, I will not be moved. Oh beautiful Messiah, my heart*

is glad for You will show me the path of life. In Your presence is absolute fullness of joy. You have promised me pleasures for evermore. You put the longing in my heart to seek You, and then You came to me and took me into Your welcoming arms, Your arms were where I belonged. You alone are my true home. Forgive me for my fears, You are all powerful and all good—yet I'm afraid. The clamor of her fears was silenced by words breathed into her soul—words only she could hear: YOU ARE FULLY KNOWN AND LOVED BY ME.

With new unshakeable reassurance, she watched as Daniel lovingly glided his hands across the dark polished wood of his pulpit. When she caught his eye, his wistful smile made clear they were recalling the same moment—when fourteen-year-old Benjamin, beaming with pride, presented his woodworking project to the family's rabbi as a birthday gift.

"I did it in shop class," he had boasted.

Benjamin was such a cute young boy, always pushing his glasses up the bridge of his nose. Daniel smiled toward Naomi and subtly mimed pushing an imaginary pair of glasses up toward his nose and they shared a sweet silent chuckle.

Pursing his lips together, Daniel chased away the nostalgic thoughts and steeled himself for moving full-on into the present. He instructed the congregation, "Read with me, 'O come, let us sing unto the LORD: let us make a joyful noise to the Rock of our salvation …'"

Others continued reading from Psalm 95 but Naomi noted Daniel's voice breaking off and then saw his glistening eyes lift heavenward. She knew what he was experiencing—the very same thing she had experienced the first time as a new Believer in Yeshua, she sat through a *Shabbat* service. Words once recited by rote year after year had overwhelmed her with their beauty. And tonight this divine appreciation was taking hold of Daniel.

Daniel wiped the tears from his eyes and reached for the glass of water always situated on a ledge inside his pulpit. "Let us welcome the Sabbath as a groom welcomes his bride."

He cleared his throat. "Dear friends, please bear with me. I am changing our usual service for the evening. I have a serious announcement to make."

While all eyes were looking expectantly to their rabbi, Naomi's eyes were drawn to the Torah cover—plush dazzling indigo velvet. With the help of Shirley, one of the older women at the Temple, Naomi had labored over the sewing and then the embroidering of this intricate design. It had some obvious flaws—the gold silk threads were a bit tangled and the design of the menorah at the center was a bit off-balance—but her husband had assured her it was perfect.

Daniel shifted his weight from one leg to the other and clasped his hands in front of his stomach and then behind his back. Finally, he spoke.

"Apologies are never easy. However, I need to apologize to every one of you sitting here tonight because I have loaded you down with burdens too heavy for any person to bear. I realize I have spoken many many times about our responsibility as Jews to take up the yoke of the law. But I now realize none of us can take up that burden—not even your rabbi."

After another swallow of water, he continued. "My first announcement is that I will be resigning as your rabbi." In response to the gasps and murmurs, Daniel extended his open palms toward his congregation, "Please, be patient and wait for me to give you an explanation."

Naomi turned around to see people looking at the person next to them or nudging the person in front of them and through the roar of the murmurings, she heard the agitated questioning. *People don't like being caught off-guard, do they?*

Daniel leaned deeper into the microphone and cleared his throat. This effectively silenced the crowd as they looked expectantly to him. "My wife and I will be available to any and all of you to come to our home and ask more questions. You see, what

I am about to tell you will startle you, and I am praying some of you will want to know more."

Daniel rubbed his neck as if trying to massage out a crick. Naomi had told him more than once, "Honey, sometimes you get this nervous gesture with your neck." He must have recalled her advice because he stopped and glanced at her.

With Daniel's lips close enough to the microphone to brush against its foam cover, he addressed his congregation. "Have you ever had an experience where in an instant everything changed? Have you ever had a revelation that made you see things differently? No, excuse me, it is more like suddenly you see with clarity … crystal clarity."

With the word clarity spoken, his jaw unclenched and the tightness around his mouth softened. "The first night we arrived in Israel, although it was late and everyone traveling with us checked into their rooms, my wife and I went to the Western Wall. I was carrying a heavy burden and believed if I prayed there at the Wall, that the burden would be lifted. While praying at the Wall, the burden I took with me *was* lifted, but not how I thought it would be. The true burden I was carrying had been that heavy yoke of the law. I need to read you something."

Naomi looked around to see if there would be a reaction as Daniel now held up a Bible which contained both the Old and the New Covenant, but before she could detect any reaction, Daniel stepped down from the platform, as was his custom. He believed it created a more casual and intimate environment for communicating with his congregation.

Once he opened his Bible to the place marked by a ribbon, he continued. "Psalm 118 always made me wonder. It says that the stone which the builders rejected has become the chief cornerstone." Looking at the congregation, he asked. "If this is referring to us as the builders, if we Jews are the builders, then who is it we have rejected?" He paused and scanned the crowd.

A few people leaned forward in their seats and raised their eyebrows. They were paying closer attention to their rabbi than Naomi had ever seen before. And it seemed from their scowls, that a few had figured where her husband was heading.

"In Yeshiva we were taught to avoid certain scriptures, one of them is the one you just heard. But why did we need to avoid these scriptures? Why do you think all year long we avoid Chapter 53 in Isaiah? Are any of you familiar with this passage in your *Tanakh*?" Their heads shook no.

"For the first time today, you will hear it. Listen and consider who Isaiah is speaking about when he says, 'He is despised and rejected of men; a man of sorrows, and acquainted with grief: and we hid as it were our faces from him; he was despised, and we esteemed him not.'"

Daniel slowly moved up the middle aisle as he continued reading. "But he was wounded for our transgressions, he was bruised for our in—"

Naomi heard the sharp intakes of breath from the congregation as she saw her husband fix his intense blue eyes on his stunned listeners. "My professors taught us that Isaiah is speaking of Israel, but I never could reconcile that being true. It is so clearly speaking about a person, and if you continue the rest of this chapter and try substituting Israel each time it says 'he' you'll see it doesn't make sense. If you would, please go home and read this chapter for yourself. Then ask if this is not about Israel, then who is it describing?" He shrugged his shoulders. "Is it your Uncle Irving?"

One demure eighty-something-year-old lady in an aisle seat, reached up to tug on Daniel's jacket. In a reedy voice, she said, "Rabbi, *genug iz genug*. Enough is enough."

He stooped down and softly said, "Please, Mrs. Schwartz, I know everyone's getting shaken up by this, but, please, give me one more minute."

Jerry, a burly man in his sixties, walked menacingly over to Daniel. "What? Someone pay you to convert so now you're trying to convert us?"

Daniel walked past Jerry and climbed back up to the podium. Naomi was amazed at the calmness of his voice. "As I announced at the beginning, I will be stepping down as your Rabbi and will arrange for a new leader." Taking one more swallow of his water, he tucked his Bible into the crook of his arm. "And again, if you want to discuss this further, please know our door is open." Down two steps, with one more to go, Daniel appeared to realize he was not finished.

"Please pray and ask God to show you the truth about our Messiah."

Naomi, her chin tucked into her chest, saw Daniel's hand suddenly reach for hers and she immediately grabbed it. He scooped her up into his loving embrace, shielding her from the murmuring crowd.

Their evening walks from the temple to their home on *Shabat* was a time Naomi always relished. A time for intimate recollections of their week and sometimes a peaceful silence, enjoying each other's presence with no need to speak a word. At such quiet times, Daniel would squeeze her hand, and she would know she belonged and was protected.

For one always wanting safety, how come I always end up taking these crazy risks.

Passing Camino Real gatehouse, the guard tipped his hat. "Good evening, Rabbi and Mrs. Cantor. Another peaceful night, isn't it?"

Both Cantors smiled and nodded. Turning the corner toward their home, Daniel suggested, "How about a few laps in the pool?"

Once home, they quickly changed into their bathing suits, and after a few laps, Daniel grabbed ahold of the pool ladder and hoisted himself up.

Surprised, Naomi asked, "You're done?" Usually he was able to go at least ten more laps than her.

His brows wrinkled, he studied her. "Naomi, you know—you understand—we will have to sell this house?"

She stopped swimming and grabbed onto a side of the pool. "Do we have to?" Slowly she nodded her head and scowled. "Yeah, I understand. After all, it's only a house." With a grin-and-bear-it smile, she used the ladder to pull herself out of the pool and sat next to Daniel on their patio sofa.

Daniel held her chin with his fingers and asked, "You know we did the right thing, don't you? Like you said, it's only a house."

"Yeah, I guess, but I love our ..." She stopped speaking and placed her head on his shoulder.

"Honey, your hair's wet. You know I hate that." He placed his hands on her shoulders and pulled himself away from her wet head.

"Oh really?" She sprung to her feet and began shaking her head close to his face, splashing him with water in every direction. "You mean like this?"

He growled, reached for a towel and the chase began, with her giggling all the way and him warning her to be careful because he would be getting even. Once they reached the bedroom, she exclaimed, "Daniel, there's a message on our machine. Will you play it for us? I'm afraid, with Dad being sick and all."

"Hello, this is Ellen Solomon with the Sun-Sentinel. A member of your synagogue called to report that something unusual happened there tonight. I'd like to interview you on this. Would you please call me back tomorrow?"

All night long Naomi was plagued with the prickling worries, the what-ifs, and the self-recrimination—only Daniel's rhythmic breathing provided some relief.

We could have had a nice peaceful life—maybe even had children— he deserves someone better than me. Yeshua, forgive me. I confess I have

7

doubted You. I know the knowledge of You and the salvation You bring are worth more than all the world can ever give me, and it was Your good pleasure to reveal Yourself to sweet Daniel. But seriously, Lord, did he have to go so far so quickly?

New words were then breathed into her soul—I have been with you through it all.

As her twenty-something years flashed before her, she realized Yeshua had been with her through it all. *You were there with me through all the rejection, all the loneliness, thinking no one would ever understand me. Through it all, You were listening. Even when I was a little girl looking into that full-length mirror and thinking I'd better face the fact that I'll never be one of the pretty ones. Then when I started accepting cheap imitations of love—even to where I gave up my baby, through it all You were there. You knew Your blood would redeem and restore a life that was bent on destruction. Through it all, Your nail-scarred hands wanted to hold me close to Your pierced side.*

Forgive me, Abba, may I honor You and not be fearful.

Chapter Two

Wooden Splinters and Ruffled Feathers

At 11:00 the next morning Naomi answered a call from their guardhouse. "Ellen Solomon is here to see you."

"Please let her in."

Naomi ran from the kitchen to the dining room where Daniel was setting out a plate of pastries. "She's here. How do I look?"

He assured her she was as beautiful as ever, but that wasn't enough for Naomi. "I'm going to change my lipstick. I don't like red-red. You know, it's too red." With a quick glimpse out their living room window, Naomi asked, "When did it start raining?"

Daniel joined her at the window. "Huh, it's starting to come down hard. Where's our umbrella?"

"Hall closet."

Naomi dashed into their bathroom to change her lipstick from flaming red to a more subdued coral while Daniel grabbed the umbrella and watched for the journalist to pull up into their circular driveway. Upon seeing the white Mercedes approach, he walked out and greeted her with his open umbrella while Naomi waited at the front door to greet the reporter. Soon the mystery would be solved as to who called the newspaper telling them about what happened at the *shul* last night. But … was that a giant black poodle coming out of the car with the reporter?

Ellen ignored the offer of Daniel's umbrella, walking past him as though he were invisible.

"Welcome," Naomi said, staring at the poodle who attempted to shake himself dry and managed to let rainwater fly in her face. *Gross, the smell of wet dog. I'm going to be sick.*

Daniel stood behind Ellen and her dog at the doorway, arching his eyebrows and shrugging his shoulders for Naomi's benefit. He closed the umbrella as Naomi ushered the woman in.

The dog pulled to get free of his leash attached to a diamond-studded collar. "I hope you don't mind, Mrs. Cantor, but I needed to take Schmendrick with me. He's been having separation anxiety lately—little accidents on the carpet and all."

"Schmen … ? I never heard a dog called that before." Naomi led the way into the dining room. "We thought this might be a good place for us to sit."

"Very good." Ellen nodded her approval as she coaxed the dog to sit at her feet.

Naomi forced a smile. "Can I get you some coffee?"

"Yes, cream with lots of sugar, please."

While Ellen's head was down retrieving her notepad and pen from her large shoulder bag, Naomi and Daniel shared a quizzical look with each other. Naomi silently mouthed "Schmendrick?" Probably not a good idea because it set Daniel off on a laughing jag. He covered it by quickly getting up from the table and explaining he wanted to help his wife in the kitchen.

Soon they both returned to the table not only with the coffee but also, on Naomi's suggestion, a bowl of water for the poodle.

"Oh, how thoughtful of you." Ellen looked down at her dog and told him, "Now thank the nice lady, Schmendrick."

With every effort to smile, Naomi placed the bowl near the animal, trying to ignore the dog's musty smell. *Revolting.* Naomi took her seat across from Ellen and next to Daniel. "I'm so curious, how'd you hear about my husband's announcement at the *shul?* I mean … it only happened last night?"

Daniel smiled. "Yes, your phone call really surprised us."

Ellen helped herself to a cheese danish and placed it on a plate set in front of her. Naomi surmised Ellen to be in her fifties, a little pudgy, but very poised and comfortable with herself. *Man, every time I've ballooned out to her size, I become total Miss Insecurity.*

After a nibble on her pastry and a sip of coffee, the woman explained. "One of the women in your congregation called me. A real pistol—she told me she had a scoop for me—really, that's the word she used." Ellen chuckled. "She must have seen too many old movies. Said if she gave me the scoop, then she would want a free ad in our weekend edition of the paper. She's a Realtor."

Daniel almost spilled his coffee laughing so hard. "Florence Greenberg."

Naomi soaked up Daniel's coffee with a handful of napkins. "She sold us this house."

Ellen, from the vantage point of the dining room, gave the house the once-over, especially fixing her attention on the Florida Room with its pool. "It's a beautiful home."

"Wait til you see the Spanish tile we have in our bathroom." Naomi squeezed Daniel's hand and smiled. "But it's only a house."

"Well perhaps 'only a house,' but I'm sure you are aware, not everyone gets to live with this exclusive an address. As I pulled into your driveway, I noticed the exquisite work of whoever you use for your landscaping."

"Actually, my wife does the landscaping. I love coming home and seeing the splashes of color she uses—they're always a bright welcome home."

Daniel and Naomi quickly turned to one another, and then swiftly toward Ellen. In unison they said, "It's only a house."

Ellen drew her chin up and nodded, holding a pen over her notepad. "So, will you now be leaving this area?"

A shrug of their shoulders was their only answer.

Clicking her pen, she asked, "Let's start with the obvious. When and how did you, a Conservative Rabbi, come to believe in Jesus?" She paused for only the briefest of moments while narrowing her eyes. "Or have you believed for a long while, but only now are admitting it to your congregation?"

Daniel leaned across the table. "Something happened in Israel. You see, our *shul* was in Israel for the last ten days. We only came back this Wednesday."

Naomi rested her chin in the palms of her hands and gazed adoringly at her husband. "Don't you just love the way he smiles? He doesn't even need to move his lips—he smiles with his eyes."

Daniel blushed, put his hand over his forehead, and shook his head. Witnessing his reaction, Naomi winced. "Wow, I'm so sorry, honey." She turned to Ellen. "Not only did I embarrass my husband, but I interrupted him, too."

Ellen's pen slipped from her fingers as she studied the couple. "What a special love you two share. I'm ..."

The woman's eyes had become moist, but soon she stiffened and leaned back against her chair. With an exaggerated grimace, Naomi said, "I'm always interrupting him and now I got us off course. My husband was about to answer your question." She turned to Daniel and nodded her head as a cue for him to continue.

"Well, as I said, something happened in Jerusalem. It was our first night there and my wife and I went to the Western Wall. While I was praying, a beautiful white bird—it seemed translucent—it flew over me and something dropped from its wings and got tangled in the knotted fringes on my prayer shawl."

"You mean the *tallit*," Ellen said as she bit into her danish.

Daniel nodded. "Not many people would know the name."

Ellen said, "I grew up in an orthodox home."

Naomi jumped in. "Me, too. I grew up sitting upstairs with my mom."

Brushing crumbs off her chin, the reporter said, "Truthfully, it was boring. All the women ever did was gossip."

Naomi nodded in agreement.

Daniel cleared his throat to get their attention, "Uh, ladies?"

"Alright, let's get back to your story—but I must say, you are a very engaging couple. I expected you to simply be … but, please, go on. Something got caught in your fringes. Was it a feather?"

"No, it was—let me show you." He reached into his pocket and brought out a wallet. From his billfold, he produced a small piece of paper, carefully unfolded it, and smoothed it out with the palm of his hand. He then read, "Come unto Me, My yoke is easy and My burden is light. I am your Messiah."

Ellen's forehead wrinkled and her eyes again narrowed. "How do you know some nut didn't … I mean …"

"Let me go back to before we arrived in Israel. You see, my wife already believed … in Jesus, that is."

Ellen's head had been down writing on her pad of paper but now looked up at Naomi. "And how did you come to believe this?"

Naomi looked toward Daniel. Should she tell the story? He placed his hand over hers. "It's up to you, sweetheart."

"It's very personal, Ellen. Let's simply say, I was hurting over something in my life, and I heard a commercial on TV which gave a number to call for exactly my problem." *Maybe one day I'll be able to speak of my abortion … but not today.* "So I called the number and the people connected with the ad told me about Jesus – I'd rather call Him by His Hebrew name, Yeshua. At first, I thought I better run away real quick, but then I realized they were worshipping our Messiah. It was like suddenly the whole meaning of being Jewish made sense—everything made sense. But—"

Ellen interrupted, "But your husband was a rabbi. Did you tell him right away or did you keep it a secret?" With her chin tilted upward and her eyes cast down upon Naomi, she asked, "From him and from his whole synagogue?"

For one brief moment Naomi looked down to avoid her interrogator but recovered soon enough and peered directly into Ellen's eyes. "Eventually he found out."

Daniel interrupted, "Yes, and I got very angry and was very cruel to her at that time."

Naomi nodded. "He told me it was like I was unclean—like an idol worshipper. It was a very painful time."

"I still loved her but thought I'd lost her. I wanted to help her see she was wrong so I began looking at her Bible, the one that had the New Testament—and I tried resisting what started becoming so clear to me—that she was right. For my whole life, I had fought the idea of any Jew converting—my parents are Holocaust survivors."

Ellen scribbled a few notes, then jutted her chin toward Naomi. "Now, Mrs. Cantor, weren't you afraid your husband, the Rabbi, would divorce you?"

"Not really … it's hard to explain, but it was like I had this calm, as if a soft voice was breathing into me, 'Just hold on, wait and see.'"

Daniel held up the small piece of white paper. "So when this note seemed to drop from the sky, I could no longer fight the truth—and once I embraced it—that Jesus is our Messiah—an incredible sense of reassurance—"

Ellen scoffed. "Incredible indeed." She again lifted her chin and fixed her eyes upon Naomi. "And is there perhaps a chance you somehow engineered for your husband to receive this 'miraculous' note?"

"Excuse me," Daniel said, "but how could she have 'engineered' something like this?" Daniel's neck turned bright red and the rush of blood was traveling up to the top of his ears.

Only one other time did Naomi ever see him like this—the time he discovered her faith in the Messiah.

Ellen clicked her pen and then pointed it at Daniel. "You know, I remember seeing a movie once. This empty can of soda, it was in Africa, the can fell from the tree to the ground and one of the tribesmen saw it fall and took it to his village. They ended up all

14

worshipping this can of soda, thinking it must be from God. After all, it came down from above."

"Charming story, Ms. Solomon. I never saw the movie. Naomi, did you?" When she shook her head, Daniel continued. "I appreciate your skepticism. Let me go back to before I received the note at the Wall. You see, before we left for Israel, as I said, I began looking at my wife's Bible. Reading the New Testament. I had trouble denying what was so clear. And after I received what you demean as a can of soda, my wife and I began reading her Bible together. And when I was no longer trying to deny what was clearly the truth, it was like scales fell from my eyes. The note that fell from above was not a soda can and my wife did not engineer anything. It was the hand of God Almighty who 'engineered' this. Of course, He doesn't engineer anything."

He reached for a danish, took a bite, and then looked intently at Ellen. "His breaking into a heart and mind that have been closed to Him, is evidence that we should never doubt Him. And the more I read about Yeshua, I realize He is the embodiment of our Jewish Scriptures."

Ellen brushed a few wisps of hair from her forehead and then folded her arms around her chest. "Perhaps, Rabbi, it was actually you who concocted this magical white note? You didn't want to lose your precious wife—"

Daniel did his characteristic clearing of his throat—which communicated to Naomi that her husband was still in control—angry, yes, but in control. "Mrs. Solomon, I know this is a volatile subject, but I had assumed this would be a—"

"Very tactful, Rabbi. Yes, it is a very, as you say, volatile subject—and I need to wrap up this interview. There is a place reserved in tomorrow's Sunday edition for my article, and Schmendrick needs to get to the groomer, so let's move on. Please tell me, what happened after your first night at the wall."

"The rest of our time in Israel, my wife and I, every evening, as soon as we got back from the tour and had dinner, we'd run into our hotel room and look at her Bible. It was as if light bulb after light bulb went on. Out of consideration for those traveling with us, I waited until we returned to America before telling my congregation. Did you know there are prophecies—"

Ellen again pointed her pen at Daniel. "Oh please, no preaching, or whatever you call it." She moved her eyes from Daniel to Naomi, then back to Daniel. "So, you were willing to give up your esteemed position, and, Mrs. Cantor, you were willing at one time to give up your husband, whom you obviously love?"

Naomi watched as Daniel looked directly into the interviewer's eyes. He was wearing what Naomi labeled "the studious rabbi face." *Wonder what he's going to ask her—you're about to be on the hot seat, lady.*

Daniel took a sip of coffee, then gently placed the cup back into the saucer—all the while his eyes peering into Ellen's. "Have you ever had anything worth giving up everything for? I think we all long for something to be that important, don't you? What if you, in an instant, found all you had been searching for your entire life? Wouldn't the cost be priceless?"

Naomi couldn't resist joining in. "I know what my husband is saying. It's like all of a sudden, the missing puzzle piece pops into place and you see the whole picture."

Ellen clicked her pen one last time and put it into her handbag which was slung over the dining room chair. She abruptly stood and yanked on the huge poodle's leash. "Schmendrick and I must go now, but before I leave, may I take a photo?"

Daniel stood and came beside Naomi. He bent down on one knee, placed his arm around her shoulder and moved his face close to hers. "How is this?"

It only took a second for Ellen to reach into the pocket of her suit jacket and produce a camera. Click. "Excellent."

Rising and heading for the front door, Daniel passed close to the dog. Schmendrick growled and Daniel, in a soft yet firm voice, asked, "Would you please command your dog to let go of my pants?"

In stunned silence, Naomi and Daniel stared at the front door as it slammed shut. Still smelling the musty dog odor, Naomi said, "Need some air freshener."

Daniel followed her into the kitchen. "Are you okay, honey?"

"I'm fine." She bolted for the dining room and nearly emptied the can of vanilla-scented air freshener on the spot where the dog had been laying. "Fine, I'm just fine."

He took the can out of her hand, placed it on the table, and led her to their comfy leather recliner in the sunken conversation pit of their home—her favorite place in the house.

Squeezed against one another in the chair, Naomi heard a deep sigh coming from Daniel. "What about you? Are you okay?"

"This rabbi needs to be a student. I have to learn how to defend what we believe. Your Bible, with those charts on the prophecies and all, that's not enough. Naomi, there are so many questions— how do I provide for us? And how do I learn …"

"The way you're feeling, that's sorta the way I felt for the last month—but now I realize, Daniel, it's like you've always taught me—that if we obey what God wants, He'll take care of us." She paused and bit her lip. "You know, as for learning and all, would you consider … maybe going to a church tomorrow?"

After a few anxious moments for Naomi, he nodded. "I can't believe I'm actually going to say yes, but we do need to find a place … a place where we might belong. But where—what church?"

"I could call Melinda—the counselor I told you about from the women's center—the one who prayed with me. Umm, I could ask her where she and her husband go. You said you wanted to meet her someday. I'm sure wherever she goes is a good place." She studied Daniel's face, and then in her panicky high squeaky voice, she asked. "Can I call her? Would that be okay"

Once she received his nod, she ran to the phone.

"Daniel, you passed where we're supposed to turn."

Without looking to check if it were clear, he quickly made an illegal U-turn on Glades Road. "Where? Fourth Avenue?"

"Yeah, you need to make a right." If only he would say something—instead he had been silent the whole ten minutes driving, and with each glance, she saw his jaw clenched—and sometimes it looked like there was a pulse from his jawline down into his throat—it was like a twitching or pulsing thing.

Naomi pointed to a limestone building, its terracotta roof providing a sunbonnet for this sand-colored structure. On the roof, there was a steeple with a cross and a church bell dangling from within. "That's it. Church of all Nations. Look at that roof. Isn't it gorgeous, Daniel?"

Daniel, his jaw slightly more clenched than it was a moment ago, replied, "You know what 'nations' means in Hebrew, don't you? Gentiles."

"But aren't we, you know, the Jews … or Israel … aren't we a nation, too?"

He pulled into a parking place, robotically turned off the engine, and stiffly walked to the passenger side. He opened the door for his wife and asked, "So, what does Melinda look like?"

"Beautiful—long red straight hair. She could have been a model. She said she and her husband would meet us at the narthex. "

He had already taken Naomi's hand, but now quickly dropped it. "The what?"

"Melinda explained it's the place right before the sanctuary. She said she'd be wearing a blue silk pants suit, and I told her I'd be wearing my green linen suit. Do I look okay, Daniel?"

"Of course. You wore it this year at Passover. Told you then how pretty you looked in it. Did you tell her we'd be the couple standing out like a bunch of sore thumbs?"

"Stop it—"

He tugged her hand, forcing her to stop walking and to look directly into his face. "Naomi, I almost wore my *kippah* and was going to bring my *tallit*. It feels wrong going into a place of worship without them. I *feel* like a sore thumb."

A gentleman about to pass them stopped and said, "You must be Naomi. I'm James. Melinda's husband. And you must be Daniel." He extended his hand to Daniel and gave him a firm handshake. "I forgot my Bible in the car." He continued to walk deeper into the parking lot, but turned back and called out to them, "Go on in, Melinda's in there waiting for you."

Maybe it was James' warm southern accent and his casual demeanor—but for whatever reason Daniel's jaw was no longer clenched and his shoulders were no longer almost high enough to touch his ears. And although earlier this morning he had insisted he needed to wear a suit and tie, after observing James' khaki pants and golf shirt, Daniel loosened his tie.

Naomi unzipped her shoulder bag and spread the sides out as she held it up to him. With a wide grin, he folded it up and released it into Naomi's custody. Mostly all those walking into the church were as casually dressed as James.

Melinda caught sight of Naomi almost immediately as she and Daniel walked through the large glass doors. Naomi left Daniel standing there as she and Melinda ran to one another and warmly hugged.

Naomi whispered into Melinda's ear, "Can't wait for you to meet Daniel."

Melinda beamed. "God has answered our prayers beyond my wildest belief. Oh my, he's quite handsome, too, isn't he?"

Naomi walked her treasured counselor over to meet her husband. Daniel stretched out his hand, which Melinda exuberantly received. "Rabbi, I am so glad to meet you."

"Please, I'd rather you didn't call me rabbi—I'm simply Daniel. And I'm very glad to meet you." He grabbed Naomi and pulled her into his chest as he looked at Melinda. "I understand you're the one to blame."

But when Naomi pulled away from Daniel's grasp ready to protest, he quickly hugged her. "Honey, you know, I'm ... that was a stupid joke. Melinda, it's a pleasure to meet you. I'm looking forward to talking more with you and your husband."

James came from behind the three, and asked, "Did I hear lunch afterwards? But for now, we better scoot on in. Man, I hate when someone takes our favorite seats."

The church was light and airy. Instead of pews, there were fully upholstered mauve chairs linked together in a theatre setting.

Walking toward their favored seats, James turned around, looked at Daniel, and pointed to the chairs. "Pink. That's what you get when you let the women do the decorating." He was quickly swatted by Melinda with the church bulletin they were given when entering the sanctuary.

Meanwhile Daniel, his arm around Naomi's waist, whispered, "Our Temple should only be as crowded—almost every seat is filled here.

Naomi observed, "And with young people, too."

Why'd I say that? Naomi, sometimes you are so dumb. But, please, Yeshua, help me help Daniel to be as excited as I am right now. Why can't he feel Your presence in this place like I do?

James led the way—third row right center. The first two seats were taken and soon the next four seats were occupied, with Melinda and Naomi seated next to each other, Daniel and James as their bookends.

Melinda leaned in to speak to Naomi, but Naomi tapped her elbow and said, "Give me a second." She then took hold of Daniel's hand. "Honey, I'm sorry. I know you were starting to get young people to come to the Temple. I'm sorry …"

"Listen to me. You have nothing to apologize for." He stroked her chin with his thumb. "First of all, it was your initiative that brought the young people. If it wasn't for you … and now here we are—"

"Yeah, in a church—which is freaking you out."

Suddenly all around them people rose from their seats and looked toward the platform—what Naomi and Daniel, in their previous life, would have called the *bimah*. Holding hands, Naomi and Daniel stood to their feet as well.

A young man, hair down to his shoulders, wearing blue jeans, a simple button-down shirt, and sneakers, walked to the baby grand piano set to the congregants' left. A young woman, as casually dressed as the pianist, followed him out and removed the microphone from its stand.

With one chord struck on the piano keys, the church was obviously familiar with the song for they immediately began singing with the vocalist. And soon arms were raised to the ceiling. Although Naomi had never witnessed anything like this before, something about it seemed so right. It was in praise of her Messiah. There was an urge on her part, but if her arms flew up, what would Daniel do? Instead, some people around were clapping in time with the music, and she chose to do the same. Daniel turned to her, smiled, and began clapping his hands as well.

After three songs, with Naomi's eyes closed, she sensed something had changed. Then came a deep-throated male voice praying. "Lord, we thank You for this time of sweet worship to You. We are humbled and honored to be called Your people—the apple of Your eye."

After the last of this prayer, Daniel abruptly sat back in his seat. She quickly sat down next to him and gave him a questioning look.

In a harsh whisper, he told her, "We, the Jewish people, are the apple of His eye—not them."

21

Melinda leaned toward them and asked, "Everything okay?"

Daniel waved his hand in a gesture of sloughing off any problem.

Melinda cupped her hand over Naomi's ear and explained, "That's our Pastor—Pastor Ling."

Standing at the podium was a young Oriental-looking man dressed in casual attire. He had a bald head and a goatee. What was she expecting? Did he have to be blonde with blue eyes or something? Church of all Nations—wow!

What was he saying? Turn to—? Melinda placed an open Bible on Naomi's lap and pointed to a particular section. "See, starting with verse 24."

As Naomi shared the open Bible with Daniel, Pastor Ling read, "Matthew 16:24-26. Then said Jesus unto his disciples, if any man will come after me, let him deny himself, and take up his cross, and follow Me. For whosoever will save his life shall lose it: and whosoever will lose his life for My sake shall find it. For what is a man profited, if he shall gain the whole world."

The Pastor closed his Bible and walked away from the podium. With his hands now in his pockets, he talked to his congregation. "Nowadays, as you Americans would say, everyone, including us Christians, we want to have our cake and eat it, too. Yeah, we believe in Jesus—but what does believe mean to you? Does it mean you believe it to the point you are willing to sacrifice whatever is asked of you? Most of you know the story of the Apostle Paul— once called Saul."

Daniel squeezed Naomi's hand. The pages in their Bible containing the story of Saul on the Damascus Road were well-worn on their Bible. The very first time they encountered it together, they had gasped –it was Daniel's story.

The Pastor continued, "When Jesus met him on the road to Damascus, Paul was faced with giving up everything, including his heritage. Did I ever tell you about my grandfather? Grandfather Heng—which by the way means persevering, and it is so fitting a name for him—he came over to the United States when he was in his 20s. As a young boy in China, he had met a Jesuit missionary, who told him about a God who loved him so much that He came to earth and died for him. Grandfather Heng said, 'She had more to tell me, and I knew she had something she wanted me to do, but then I was told 'hurry, we must pack our things immediately.' You see, they were coming to America. I remember sitting on Grandfather Heng's lap, his face would crinkle up in this big toothless smile."

A screen now projected a photograph of an elderly toothless Chinese man, smiling happily. "Grandpa would tell me, 'I couldn't forget, I needed to know what missionary wanted me to do. Then on streets of New York City I see young woman handing out little books to people. I somehow know, here's what I'm looking for. I go to her and say, please you finish what missionary started.' My Grandfather then repeated a prayer after her and accepted Jesus as his Savior. It's because of Grandfather Heng I grew up in a Christian home. And you know what? He was rejected by his family. He told me he was thrown out of the house, lost his job in a restaurant, and I guess never got the money to get his teeth fixed!"

The Pastor laughed along with his congregation and continued, "But because of his being willing to sacrifice, because he picked up his cross, my parents, their children, and now my children, all are growing up knowing the love of Christ. I want to ask you, what are you holding on to? Yes, picking up and holding onto the cross, you might get a few splinters."

James double-parked in front of the Sticky Bun café and turned to the back of his sedan and explained to Daniel and Naomi, "Melinda will get us a booth—we like the booth in the corner by the window—and this place will be packed any minute now. I'll park behind here and meet you inside."

Naomi could tell Daniel was not pleased with this arrangement, but James had insisted they leave their car in the church's parking lot. Before Daniel could voice his objection, James explained, "I'll drive you back over there after lunch."

When Melinda slid out of the front seat, Daniel took Naomi's hand and helped her out. Good thing they stepped onto the sidewalk lickety-split since James whizzed by them immediately.

Melinda smiled apologetically at them. "Sorry." She then hustled through the door and made her way to the booth situated in the corner by the window. Before her husband arrived, Melinda leaned in to Naomi and whispered, "I really am sorry about James driving off like that, but you know, we all have our quirks, don't we?"

"We call them *shticks*—or *shtickla*. Don't worry."

"Thanks, Naomi. Speaking of quirks, James likes sitting on the outside, so how about you and I sit on the inside together and our husbands can sit across from each other?"

Perfect arrangement—now Naomi might have an opportunity to talk with Melinda like she'd been yearning to for over a month now—so much to catch up on.

After both women were in the booth, Melinda turned to Daniel. "Rabbi, how did you like our service?"

Trying to hide her maddening impatience to hear his answer, Naomi grabbed a menu sitting on their table and kept her eyes glued to it—all the while holding her breath. *Oh, please, Lord, let him have loved it as much as I did.*

Before Naomi could hear Daniel's answer, James arrived and slipped into the booth. He told Melinda, "He doesn't like being called Rabbi. Told me to call him Daniel." With that, he winked toward Daniel.

Melinda tilted her head to one side. "But, why not? I was told rabbi meant teacher. Is that right?"

Daniel smiled and nodded. "The only thing is, Melinda, this teacher needs to be a student right now."

Both James and Melinda said, "I understand." James then added, "It must be tough."

Naomi was about to jump out of her skin. "But what about the service? Did you like it, Daniel?"

He took hold of her hand which was clutching onto his arm, kissed her fingers, and said, "Yes. But I was wondering, did Melinda call her pastor about us?" Seeing their confused faces, he said, "What? Am I supposed to have not noticed that the message was directed at both of us?"

Melinda twirled her hair in her fingers and laughed. "I remember the first time I went to church—it wasn't even Church of All Nations back then—but it seemed like the message was always aimed directly at me."

James leaned into Daniel. "Yeah, me, too. Happens a lot as a matter of fact. One time I had had a fight with my beautiful wife and out of the mouth of the preacher was exactly what I needed to hear." James rubbed his closely cropped head. "The sermon wasn't even over, and I whispered to her, 'Babe, I'm sorry'."

A barrel-chested man, seated in a wheelchair, wheeled over from a nearby table. He pulled on his brakes and stared at Daniel. "Is this—?"

James extended his hand to the new arrival. "Hey, Ray, good to see you. How've you been?"

"Been busier than a centipede at a toe counting contest." When James looked askance, Ray said, "Okay, how about this one? I'm busier than a one-armed wallpaper hanger. You like that one better?" Ray pushed his large eyeglasses further back on his face and with a playful twinkle, said, "Missed you at Sunday School today."

"We had guests." James looked toward Naomi and Daniel. "Ray, I want to introduce you to—"

"I know who they are," Ray interrupted. "These two are the reason I wheeled myself over here." He extended his hand toward Daniel. "I'm Ray, the Director of Programs at the church."

25

Melinda explained, "He does just about everything at our church … a man of many hats everyone says."

The man peered into Daniel's eyes. "I read about you in the Sun-Sentinel this morning. I got so excited, I spilled my coffee." Ray tugged at his shirt and pointed toward a large stain near his front pocket. "See. and the coffee was hot, too. June wanted me to change before coming to church, but I said, nah, no one looks at me anyway."

Naomi's eyes widened. "We haven't even seen the newspaper yet."

"Oh ho," Ray said with a chuckle. "Got it at my table." He unlocked the brakes and wheeled off to his table. He zipped back, newspaper in hand. "Reporter was pretty snarky, wasn't she? Guess you really ruffled her feathers. Noticed her name was Solomon."

Naomi used all her willpower not to snatch the paper from the man but instead allowed her husband to receive it from Ray. She leaned over Daniel's shoulder and said, "Well, the picture is okay at least."

James commented, "Women!"

Holding the paper so Naomi could read, Daniel asked, "What do you mean 'snarky'?"

"Oh, like when you were telling her about what happened to you in Israel—which was really amazing—but our God is amazing, isn't he?" Ray reached for a glass of water sitting in front of Daniel. "Do you mind?"

"Not at all."

After a swallow of water, Ray explained. "When you told about Israel at the wall, instead of simply quoting you, she writes—" Ray stretched out his hand toward the newspaper. "Let me see it for a minute." He scanned the article. "Ah ha—there it is." He inched his chair closer to Daniel and pointed his finger. "There, see where she says 'he claims'—and I think she did that several other times. You get it, don't you? She says 'claims' like it's her wink-wink to the reader, saying 'the guy's lying.'"

Naomi asked, "Can we keep the paper? Would you mind?"

"Sure why not? So, how do you fine folks know each other?"

Naomi could feel the blood rushing to her face. To hide the blush, she nuzzled into Daniel's shoulder.

Melinda looked at Naomi and Daniel and quickly said, "Well, what's really interesting is how Ray and my husband know each other. They were in the marines together. Stationed in Pensacola, and then they both ended up here in Boca Raton, at the same church."

Both Ray and James pumped their arm and in chorus, sang out, "Oorah."

Ray released the brake on his chair and was about to push off again. "Go ahead and keep the paper. But I'll tell you, I think this was a divine appointment that we met. After reading about you this morning, I thought I gotta talk to this guy. Would you be willing to meet me at the church this week some time?" He reached into his shirt pocket and pulled out a business card. "Got a proposal for you." He handed Daniel the card and whisked away.

Melinda smiled and reached across the table to place her hand on Naomi's. "Hey, hope you know you don't need to worry about people asking how we met. You can always say 'at a Bible study.'"

Does James know though? Did she—?

Melinda now leaned across the table and whispered, "Even James hasn't asked. Guys are not curious like us—sometimes it's a godsend."

Naomi now overheard James telling Daniel, "You should call Ray this week. He's an inspiration to everyone and seems like he has something special he wants to talk to you about."

By the following day, Naomi had reminded Daniel at least five times to call Ray. After the third time when he told her to "stop pushing me," she tried to stop, but she kept thinking it could be important. After all, James had told her husband that it seemed Ray had something "special" to talk to him about. What if it had to do with a job?

The next morning, Naomi awoke to see her clock read five a.m. Going back to sleep was impossible. Thoughts swirling around in her head. How were they going to support themselves now? Could they sell their house without a realtor and make more money? Maybe they'd move back to New York, or even to New Jersey. What options were there for them? Would her parents help? She doubted it—to them they were now heathens. Why hadn't Daniel called that Ray guy immediately after they got home?

If it were up to me, I would have called as soon as we got home.

And there was Daniel peacefully sleeping.

She really hadn't ever worried about money that much. The only time she could really remember worrying was when she first moved to New York City, but Mom and Dad bailed her out, at least until she got that waitressing job. And once she began to turn on the charm, her tips were envied by the other wait staff. Then before she knew it, she was earning money as an actress. That even made her father say, "I'm proud of you," especially when her floor wax commercial started airing. Her father told her, "You're doing good, kid." He loved it when the townfolk said, "Hey, Saul, is that your Naomi I saw on TV?"

Hmmm, why am I reminiscing about my past life? I'm happier now for sure. It's just the money thing and Daniel never asked me if he should resign that quickly. When he made the announcement and resigned, we hadn't even unpacked from Israel.

She was most certainly thrilled that they were now united in their faith—it was exquisite—their time in Israel breathtaking. YET why couldn't he have talked this over with her, and maybe talked about consequences and options before blurting it out at the *shul*?

She couldn't possibly earn money now as an actress and Daniel, other than being a rabbi, his only other job was working at his father's furniture store. And to top it off, now they were like a bunch of outcasts … except at church yesterday where she had a strong sense of belonging. Belonging—what a beautiful word. She rolled over in bed to gaze at the man God had given her.

Melinda had once suggested to Naomi that it would be good to memorize scripture—to "hide His word in your heart." This discipline became very dear to Naomi, having committed to memory several psalms and several chapters from the Gospel of John. Since she didn't seem able to go back to sleep, she decided to review Psalm 37. It was the first thing she had ever memorized and was at a time Daniel was not speaking to her because of her new-found faith. When she reached verse 4, "delight yourself in the Lord and He will give you the desires of your heart," she remembered how whenever she got to that verse, she would pray, "Lord, I am delighting in You, but the desire of my heart is for my husband to know you."

If he could perform that miracle, then I guess I should trust Him to provide for us today and even tomorrow?

Naomi quietly made her way out of the bed and noiselessly dressed. After a quick cup of coffee, she drove to the nearest Publix. Several hours later, she was pouring boiling water into a bowl which contained a mixture of prunes and mushrooms and was so intensely preoccupied that she was unaware of Daniel having approached. Leaning over the countertop studying the recipe, she suddenly felt arms wrapped around her waist followed by a playful nibble at her neck.

"You're making my favorite—bigos!" He swung her around for a full-frontal hug.

"I know it's kinda like crazy—ninety-something degrees outside and I'm making a stew—like it was winter."

"It'll be perfect. We'll turn up the A/C."

She walked over to the stove and picked up a large wooden spoon. "I have to stir the onions and cabbage."

Grabbing the bottle of wine sitting on the countertop, he offered, "Let me pour the wine in. You found Mogen David's Ruby Grapefruit—I don't believe it."

Naomi watched as he splashed more than the recipe called for. "No, that's too—." With the sizzling sound as the wine hit the pot and the fragrance filled the air, she held her tongue. The only thing she could imagine making her husband this jubilant would be if she could say, "I'm pregnant." *Oh, if only.*

"What kind of meat are you going to use?"

"The leftovers from our hamburgers the other night."

He waited until she placed the meat into the pot and stirred the concoction a few times. He then took her by the hand. "Can we sit down for a few minutes and talk?"

"Of course."

"I know I told your friends the other day to not call me rabbi, but if I were to be honest, I don't know who I am anymore. I don't believe it was ever for the status or the title, but there was an identity with the title, and the title came with a purpose. Your friend Melinda asked what I thought about the service—I felt like answering, 'excuse me, but what am I supposed to compare it with?'"

"Do you wish you could like rewind the tape and still be the rabbi at Temple Beth Shalom?"

"No, absolutely not. I'm not going to run away from what I know is the truth—you didn't. But I do still need to think of how I'm going to provide for us—oh, by the way, James gave me the name of a realtor—it's his sister." He studied her face for a moment, then asked, "You okay with that?"

She turned her face from his peering eyes. "I'm fine. I better go check on the pot."

"It smells delicious."

Holding the wooden spoon, she said, "Come taste."

As he savored the hot stew, she said, "You know I can still remember Mom using a spoon like this. Every time I use it, I feel like I'm following in her footsteps. Crazy, huh? It's only a wooden spoon, but …"

"No, not crazy. I remember my Mom would offer Dad a taste the same way." Imitating his mother's thick Polish accent, he said, "Stefan, come taste. And then Dad would say the same thing I'm going to tell you—it's delicious. We have so many treasured traditions, probably from our parents bringing them over from the old country."

With one short beat, they looked at each other. "Daniel, what about your parents? Mine at least know—they want to disown me, but they know. How are we going tell yours?"

"I can't think about that right now. But let me ask you something? What do you think the guy in the wheelchair wants?"

Naomi, trying to appear nonchalant, shrugged. "I don't have a clue. Why don't you … maybe call him."

He reached into his pocket but his hand came back empty. "I thought I put his business card in here. This is the shirt I was wearing yesterday, isn't it?

"Yeah, I think so." She feigned accidentally finding the card as she moved her head toward the kitchen table. "Oh, Daniel, here it is." Last night while he slept, she had removed it from his pocket fearing he would somehow put the shirt in with the laundry and it would get ruined. She now casually walked to the table, picked up the card, and handed it to him. "I don't know how it got here, but here it is."

"Maybe he knows how new all this is for me and he's offering to guide me along—or something like that. I mean when someone came to the *shul*, I'd always offer to help them get acclimated." He slumped into the kitchen chair, biting his lip and shaking his head. "Will I always be relating everything to who I used to be? Do you ever miss being an actress? I mean there was a time that was your whole life, and it was your identity."

It was true she did from time to time think about her career, just like this morning, and with it would come an uncomfortable yearning. But never would she tell him. Before she could give him a plausible denial, Daniel cried out, "Naomi, look." He quickly walked to her and placed the card so close to Naomi's face that it tapped her nose. "Do you see it?"

"Daniel, how do you expect me to see it when it's …"

She was about to take it from his hand to see for herself when he slapped it down on the countertop. "Do you see it? Klein, his last name is Klein. Ray is Jewish."

"Wow! That must be why he wanted you to call him."

"Someone who will understand our, I don't know what you'd call it—culture shock?"

"Do you remember? Yesterday he said when he read about us in the newspaper, he almost spilled his coffee? Daniel, call him." Oops, he was already calling.

"Church of all Nations. How may I serve you today?"

"Hello, my name is Daniel Cantor. I would like to speak to Ray Klein, please."

"Oh, Mr. Cantor, Monday is the day our clergy take off. But I believe I have a note from Brother Ray. Hold on a moment." After a short pause, with Daniel and Naomi communicating with each other with their smiles and gazes, the receptionist came back on the line. "Mr. Cantor, I have a note here that says if you were to call, I should contact Brother Ray, and tell you he will call you right back. If that will be all right with you, please give me your phone number?"

"Yes, of course. 561-283-3336. Thank you." He turned to Naomi as he ended the call.

"She said he'd call me back. Meantime, I'm starving. Whatcha got til the bigos is ready?"

"I can get you a bagel. With veggie cream cheese?"

He nodded but before she had finished smearing the bagel with the spread, their phone rang.

"Hello."

"Hey, is this the rabbi?"

Naomi could hear Ray's loud and cheerful voice as if she herself were holding the phone to her ear. Daniel placed his hand over the mouthpiece and cleared his throat. After what felt like an unendurably long wait to Naomi, her husband finally responded, "Yes, this is Daniel Cantor."

"Gotcha. Listen, you want to meet me at the restaurant we were in yesterday? Or you could come to the church tomorrow—whichever would be more comfortable for you."

"The restaurant would be nice."

Naomi held the knife in midair, and threw a questioning glance at Daniel. He shook his head and pointed his chin at the bagel and then moved his eyes to the refrigerator. She followed his *instructions* and put the bagel and cream cheese in the refrigerator.

When both Daniel and Ray agreed they could be there within an hour, Ray added, "And if Mrs. Cantor wants to come, that'd be great, too."

Naomi, with her uncanny ability to read a situation before it materializes, knew she would need to hurry and dress (in something suitable, of course) for an important meeting. Therefore, when Daniel apologized for the short notice he gave her, she had already decided what she would wear.

Rushing to the bedroom, she yelled back, "I'm going to put on that pants suit—you know, the one with the sailor collar."

"How did you ..." He shrugged one shoulder and followed her to change his clothes as well. "You know, this thing of yours, knowing before you're even told, it's kinda spooky, you know?"

"Yeah, I know, it spooks me out, too, sometimes."

Before leaving their home, Daniel, straightening his tie, admitted, "I'm nervous. I don't know why. I guess I'm hoping—."

"Me, too."

Chapter Three

February 1980

*a*s a young girl, Naomi's parents would take her into the city to visit Aunt Ida, and even once or twice to see a Broadway show. Today, as a young adult, it was a different story. Never ever did she find Manhattan intimidating until now. It moved with such an intense electrifying speed with just too many sensations all at once. No one talked about panic attacks back then, but if they did this small-town girl would have been a great case study. Those first few weeks in New York City could have been enough to cause her to hightail it back home. Home. Safe. Naomi, however, never really liked safe. And all her life she existed as the outsider, so really feeling isolated was nothing new to her.

Her parents older than all her friends. Fat. Frizzy hair. Because her father wanted his daughter to be popular, she learned to act—to cover up the pain of rejection, all the while raging resentment building to a rolling boil.

So, okay, now she's an outsider in this frightening confusing city. Nothing like a defiant "I'll show them" spirit to propel one past their fears. What was the option? Return to her small hometown in the Catskills? Ellenville—where everyone knew she had taken the Greyhound into Manhattan? She had to lug two large suitcases into the bus since Dad wouldn't drive her, furious after having paid a year's tuition for her college—all the way in Pittsburgh no less. Dad had said she had to go to college, but she wanted to start a career in professional theatre. The compromise was a college in Pittsburgh which offered a degree in theatre arts while apprenticing with a professional theatre company. But after a little over a year, the itch to be right in the thick of it overpowered her.

"In the middle of the semester …?" Dad had fumed, his cigar smoke choking both her and her mother. With Naomi's pleading (or perhaps demanding) and her mother's pleading, Dad agreed to help her financially. "Just once, this check and that's it, for your *cockamamie* idea."

So here she was going for her first audition and arriving late. Would she ever figure out these *cockamamie* subways? Her first audition, starting out from the West Village and thinking she was heading for midtown, how did she end up in Greenpoint, Brooklyn? Over an hour late for the audition, she walked into the darkened theatre and saw a woman seated at a table. Actresses were lining up to hand something to this woman. Naomi tried nonchalantly to spy out what exactly they were turning in. Good grief! It was these fancy glossy pictures of themselves, and then she noticed there was something typed on the back. Slowly, as unobtrusively as possible, she slunk out of the theatre, having no idea how one managed to get such a photo.

Should she just give up—go back to Ellenville—or she could make Dad happy and go back to college? But college was still all about acting.

Miss Hawksley! It's because of her gym teacher she needed to stay in this crazy city and why she needed to succeed. Be on stage and wow the audiences. She could do it. All through junior high and into high school, Miss Hawksley hated Naomi. As the gym teacher, she made Naomi the booby prize for every kickball team BUT after she saw Naomi playing Anne Frank in the high school drama production, suddenly Naomi Goldblatt was her favorite athlete. And even her Dad—the only time she ever heard him say "I'm proud of you," was also after Anne Frank.

And could anything match the excitement she felt when she was awarded this starring role? She had more lines than anyone else. And it was easy—she could easily let her imagination soar and become Anne Frank. Ultimately, it was only through acting that she could experience acceptance and run from the specter of rejection.

New York City—if you can make it here, you can make it anywhere.

Chapter Four

When You Were Jewish

*I*t seems the Tulip Café was not only popular for Sunday breakfasts, as they had witnessed the other day, but today an early lunch crowd filled every table. Thankfully Ray had arrived earlier and wheeled himself over to them. "Follow me, folks. I have a table there in the corner. It'll give us some privacy."

Once at the table, Daniel pulled out a chair for Naomi, and before seating himself, he vigorously shook Ray's hand. "You're Jewish—you can't imagine how much—

"Oh ho," Ray interrupted and chuckled. "You thought I was Jewish! Actually, you wouldn't believe how many people see my name and they think I'm a Jew. Hate to disappoint you, but I'm German. My full name is Reynard—actually a German would call me Reinhard, but my parents suggested I tell everyone my name's simply Ray—prejudice and all." As Daniel sank into a chair, Ray peered into his face. "I read where your parents were in the Holocaust."

"Seems you have the advantage—you know all about me, and I know—" Daniel looked up as a waitress arrived at their table. He turned to Naomi. "Honey, what will you have?"

She leaned into Daniel and whispered, "I'm not that hungry." She quickly scanned the menu. "This sounds good, the fruit and cottage cheese dish."

Daniel, not as good with speedreading as Naomi, asked the waitress, "Do you have a hamburger?"

She nodded and asked, "French fries?"

"Yes, please—and a chocolate shake."

Daniel must be really hungry—or nervous. There goes my special dinner with the bigos tonight. Have to freeze it, I guess. Is this my imagination, or are people really staring at us?

It seemed they not only were staring but were also whispering among themselves. Naomi asked Ray, "Does everyone here read the Sun-Sentinel?"

Ray nodded. "Pretty much—why you ask?"

The waitress swiveled her head back to Naomi and then to Daniel. "That's where I saw you two before—you were in yesterday's paper."

Ray cleared his throat and drew the waitress's gaze back to him and handed her the menu. "Charlene, I'll have my regular."

The waitress walked away, glancing back at Daniel and Naomi. Ray shrugged his shoulders and smirked. "It doesn't take much to become a celebrity around here, does it? But now let's continue. You were about to say you know nothing about me, right?"

"You can understand, I'm sure," Daniel leaned across the table. "I'm especially curious about this proposal you mentioned."

Ray unfolded his napkin and placed it on his lap. "Let me ask you something—now that you've converted and resigned from your synagogue, do you know what you'll be doing?"

This startled Naomi. Melinda had assured her she hadn't converted—but just came to believe in the Messiah. Naomi observed the tightening of her husband's jaw, but was relieved that after a few short tense moments, he answered Ray. "No, no plans—I wish I did, but no, I don't. The only definite plan is to sell our house." He patted Naomi's hand, "Which I hate doing to my wife."

Ray's index finger shot upward. "Aha." He then pointed the same finger toward Daniel. "Hebrew. What do you think? Huh? I assume you can read and speak Hebrew?"

40

With his eyebrows furrowed, Daniel answered, "*Ken.* That's Hebrew for yes."

Ray's eyes widened, as he vigorously nodded. "Yes, just the inflection in your voice—I love the sound of it. Yes indeed." He shook a packet of sugar, ripped it open, and poured it into his coffee, all the while his eyes fixed on Daniel. "How would you like to teach Hebrew to us Gentiles?"

"I'd love to."

"Thought you would. Now, we couldn't pay enough to keep you in your posh little neighborhood, but … you see, our church is starting a K through twelve school, and then, of course, we have our adult classes—like the Sunday School your friends James and Melinda attend."

"Mr. Klein, I'm somewhat apprehensive. How can I teach anyone anything? Yes, Hebrew, of course, but if you're talking about teaching from the Bible … maybe someday that'll happen."

Ray's face crinkled with his broad smile. "Well, let's start with this—Mr. Klein was what they called my father. I'm Ray, please." His fork in his hand, Ray wagged it toward Daniel. "You call me Mr. Klein ever again, I'm going to call you Rabbi—deal?"

"Deal. I can't imagine anything I would love more than one day teaching the Bible, but even my *Tanakh*—what you would call the Old Testament—now that I know we missed the Messiah, I need to relearn everything. The Hebrew—yes, I'd love to teach it to people in your church."

His fork still in midair, Ray responded. "You know, something else I'm thinking … our church is part of the Baptist denomination, and I bet you never heard about the Baptist Missionary Association when you were Jewish."

Naomi stopped chewing and cut her eyes toward Daniel to see if he had a reaction. Just as she had feared—his neck was turning bright red, with the flush moving up to his cheeks.

Naomi quickly jumped in. "Melinda told me we're still Jewish. Was she wrong?"

Ray said, "Well, I guess I stand corrected. But, I tell you what, I wish I were Jewish. You people are very special."

"Why? Do you wish you were exterminated like my grandparents?" When Daniel heard Naomi's sharp intake of breath and saw her push back against her chair, he reached over to Ray's hands which were now tightly gripping the armrests of his wheelchair. "I'm sorry, I just didn't know how to respond to what you said."

Ray smiled and in turn patted Daniel's hands. "I probably need to apologize to you. I'm sure I said something dumb. My wife tells me I do that sometimes."

"No, I wouldn't say dumb—but I guess it's a good thing to have a wife who can tell you the truth, huh?" Daniel tilted his head toward Naomi and gave her a playful elbow nudge. As the tension seemed to subside, Daniel said, "I would like to ask a favor, if you don't mind?"

Ray leaned forward and nodded. "Shoot."

"Your Pastor yesterday, in his sermon, spoke about all of you being the apple of God's eye. Please tell him that it is the Jewish people, only the Jewish people, who are called the apple of God's eye. Would you mind conveying that message to him?"

Naomi wanted to quickly say something to smooth things over, but before she could, she bit into a cherry and was surprised her teeth encountered a pit. She delicately grabbed a napkin and placed it over her mouth to dispose of it, and then quickly said. "I'm sorry, Ray, but please understand my husband didn't mean …"

Ray turned to Daniel. "You haven't touched your hamburger." As Daniel then lifted the hamburger bun and squirted ketchup inside, Ray continued. "It might not be the same thing at all, but when I ended up in this wheelchair and was trying to adjust to it, people were saying some of the dumbest things to me. Like I said, it's not the same thing at all—just some situations invite stress. Well, that said, let me take a bite of my grilled cheese and you enjoy your burger—and then I got something else to talk to you about."

Daniel nodded and took a generous bite from his burger while Naomi carefully bit into another cherry.

Ray, chewing on his sandwich, asked, "Can I take a few of your French fries?"

"*Ken*," Daniel answered.

Ray took a handful of fries. "I really should order them for my-self, but June is always harping me about my cholesterol. So, about this something else I want to talk to you about." He paused and widened his eyes. "Sure you didn't know this, but we actually have a Mission to the Jews. Got your attention, didn't I?. Hear me out. We would pray about it—that's the important thing—praying to know God's will—and if it turned out it was His will, then there's always the possibility of a scholarship to a Bible College. Huh? Huh? Sound good?"

Ray turned toward Naomi whose eyes had widened and grinned at Daniel. "Look at your wife's face! I get the feeling she is excited about the possibility?" Studying Daniel's face, he commented, "And you? You don't look so excited."

"My wife's a former actress. I think for her, it sounds like an exciting role to play." He turned to Naomi, yet her eyes were down-cast and averting contact with his. With his fingers, he lifted up her chin and asked, "Am I right? You're already seeing yourself in a pith helmet." When she still did not respond to his cajoling, Daniel dropped his fingers from her chin but squeezed her hand instead. "Ray, I'm sorry. I didn't mean to ... it's just I never imagined seeing my name associated with the title missionary."

"Look, you said you didn't know anything about me. And, you know, too much talk about you anyway—I like talking about myself. So, what can I tell you? I know what you want to ask about—it's what everybody wonders about when they first see me." While helping himself to another French fry, Ray explained, "I end-ed up in a wheelchair after coming back from Vietnam. Can you believe it? Yeah, I made my way through the whole war and funny thing, I get back home and into a car accident. Return to my beautiful bride, my little June bug. We were married two months before the Marines ended up shipping me off to Nam, and now she's got a husband in a wheelchair. But I tell you what—it's because of these wheels, I'm now rolling with Jesus. This is what it took for me to see I'm not such a big shot like I always thought I was."

Naomi sat through the rest of lunch with her stomach in knots. She wanted so much to ask Ray more questions—a missionary ... a mission to the Jews ... Daniel going to Bible College. She waited and waited, but Daniel never pursued any of this. It was like she and Daniel were orbiting two different spheres and instinct told Naomi it would not be appropriate for her to bring the discussion back to what had intrigued her.

The meal over, Ray insisted on paying the check. Finally, Daniel agreed and asked, "Can I help you to your car? How do you—?"

"My June bug is across the street—she loves spending time at the library. I'll wheel myself over there."

Shaking hands, Ray said, "Listen, I'm sorry for anything I said that—well, you know, wasn't right. In all my years of travel, I never met a converted Jew before. But you betcha I'll tell Pastor Ling what you said about your 'apple of His eye' comment. Of course, he is the Pastor and I gotta respect his authority."

Naomi waited for Daniel to say something gracious, but he didn't. *Time to stop being the timid little woman.* Naomi put her hand out to Ray and said, "Ray, it was a pleasure meeting you. Maybe we can start going to your Sunday School class."

"Well, thank you very much, young lady. Oh, one suggestion—and only if you like—but I found when I first became a Christian, listening to Christian radio really helped me. The music was beautiful, but I tell you, the teaching I got from there, it was like going to seminary. The best one around here is 101.2 FM."

Naomi waited, but Daniel said nothing. She thanked Ray and then decided, appropriate or not, she would plunge into it. "And maybe we can ask you some more questions about the missionary thing and the Bible college ... maybe later."

Ray turned to Daniel, but Daniel did not meet his eyes.

EIGHT YEARS EARLIER

The Admission Committee Chairman, Rabbi Glassman, opened the door for Daniel, shook his right hand and patted him on his left shoulder. He smiled with his mouth but not with his eyes. The Rabbi walked back to his chair, which was at the center of a long table, and pointed his chin to indicate where Daniel was to sit.

Across from this seat sat five other men, all in black suits, a pin on each lapel designating that they were on this auspicious committee. Daniel, dressed in his usual khaki pants, a plain white shirt, and his blue blazer, took a quick glance down at his sockless feet. Loafers without socks had been a part of his comfort zone for years now. Not knowing what to do with his hands, he shoved them into his pockets as he sat. "Gentlemen."

The man seated to Rabbi Glassman's left warmly smiled and introduced himself. "Rabbi Hirsch. I am very glad to meet you, Daniel." This Rabbi, looking to be about 15 years older than Rabbi Glassman, smiled with his eyes along with his mouth. Waving his hand to the right of the Committee Chair, he stated, "Please meet Rabbi Green, Rabbi M—."

Rabbi Glassman cut in, turning to Rabbi Hirsch, "Thank you, but I will introduce our committee."

"Yes, of course," apologized the elder rabbi.

Rabbi Glassman, while pouring water from a carafe into his glass, pointed to the three men to his right. "Mr. Cantor, please say hello to Rabbi Lefkowitz, Rabbi Mendel, and Rabbi Gold. They are a part of our distinguished committee."

Daniel acknowledged these three men who gave a quick nod in his direction but quickly continued their conversation amongst themselves.

The Chairman now turned back to Rabbi Hirsch, and asked, "Would you be kind enough to introduce Rabbi Weitzman?"

Rabbi Hirsch lifted an eyebrow toward Daniel and said, "Can be a rather somber, perhaps even intimidating experience, can't it?" He then turned to a tall wiry man and said, "Please meet the very distinguished Rabbi Weitzman."

Rabbi Weitzman stood and quickly gave a mock bow to Daniel and then to the other five men. "I am honored to be among these even more distinguished men." Taking his seat, he commented, "We do need to lighten up a bit, don't you think?"

Daniel wasn't quite sure, but he believed he saw a wink. He was tempted to wink back but knew better. He only prayed that Rabbi Weitzman would be his professor—if he was accepted.

Rabbi Hirsch, in a voice sonorous enough for a radio announcer, told Daniel, "We were quite impressed with the scores from both your Hebrew and from your textual analyses."

Rabbi Glassman broke in, "We understand you will be graduating Columbia this year. Please tell us about your major at the University and your decision to now work toward ordination with our Rabbinical School."

Daniel leaned forward with eagerness. His discomfort and doubts regarding his attire faded away—he relished explaining the passion behind his decision-making. "My major has been in liberal arts with an emphasis on English literature. My plans had been after graduation this year to enter law school. I will be truthful with you—I felt no passion to be a lawyer, it just seemed that's what my parents had hoped for."

Rabbi Weitzman grinned as he enthusiastically said. "Yes! Passion—good for you—it's sometimes lacking here—we need youthful passion, don't we rabbis?" Although he had turned to his colleagues, only Rabbi Hirsch made eye contact with him and smiled. "Please continue, I look forward to hearing more."

"I look forward to telling you. I wanted to please my parents but, you see, my parents are both Holocaust survivors, and all my life, ever since learning about their history, I have wanted to not only cling to my Judaism but convey the importance that our people must also cling—if our faith is worth dying for, then it's worth living for, as well. Today we have more Jewish people converting, not clinging to their God-given faith, but assimilating with the rest of the world. I believe I can inspire others to appreciate who we are as a people and, if anything, inspire the goyim to convert to our religion. When I explained this to my parents, my mother and father were very happy and now support my decision."

Rabbi Glassman turned to Rabbi Hirsh. "If you don't mind, I would like to address the candidate myself." He now turned to Daniel. "What I am very curious about is how you became so proficient in Hebrew. I see from your application you only studied Hebrew with your local rabbi just to prepare you for your Bar Mitzvah. Yet your score on our Hebrew placement exam displayed a command of the language which would be envied by scholars having studied professionally for years."

"After my Bar Mitzvah, I simply couldn't stop learning— the elementary study only whetted my appetite. After all Hebrew will be the language we speak when we are enjoying the World to Come. So why not be proficient in this world?"

All ten rabbis arched their eyebrows, turned to the other, and nodded.

Chapter Five

A Peek Into History

Driving home from the Tulip Café Naomi and Daniel withdrew into the shadowy place where fears disguise themselves as reality. Daniel knew his wife wanted to jump at Ray's offer—actually he feared any offer would sound good to her and he would somehow be propelled forward because of her enthusiasm—*no, because of her insecurity. How could I share my thoughts with such an insecure person?*

And in Naomi's private universe she began questioning her husband's faith. Did he really believe in Yeshua? Yeah, he had head knowledge, but for her it was so much more. The very moment she reached out and spoke her Redeemer's Name, night became morning. He had embraced her in a fullness this earth never gave her. Yes, for her it was emotional, spiritual, and intellectual—but for Daniel? If he hasn't really experienced the abundant joy and peace Messiah gives, then of course, he would take offense at Ray's comments. Yeah, she was still Jewish, not some converted Jew turned Gentile—but she loved her Savior and would give up anything and everything for Him. So what if someone calls her converted? That's their problem, not hers. It's just ignorance.

Nothing is more lonely than being with the one who is supposed to vanish the loneness—marriage is supposed to chase it away and create oneness. An image flashed—she was sitting on a bed, playing cards spread out in front of her—solitaire, solitaire, and more solitaire.

The quiet screamed to the point Daniel had to say, "Naomi, we need to talk."

Maybe it was the dreadful memory of those days playing solitaire that made her words sound so harsh. "You embarrassed me, Daniel." In a poor attempt to imitate her husband, she deepened her voice and said, 'Tell your pastor—."

Jamming on the brakes at a yellow light, he turned to face her. "And you're ready to jump into all of this, just like you did with Judaism when I first met you. I'm sorry, Naomi, but my being Jewish means too much to me."

"Oh, of course, Daniel, I'm just a stupid shallow actress, right?"

Both unhappy with hearing their own angry voice, they chose silence for the rest of their drive home. Once in their driveway, Daniel put the car in park while Naomi unbuckled her seatbelt, turned her body toward the car door anticipating the usual—he would turn off the motor and walk around to her. She took for granted today would be no different.

However, on this day Daniel allowed the motor to continue running and hit the steering wheel with his fist. "When you *used* to be Jewish! When I *used* to be Jew …! I'll never stop—*we*'ll never stop being Jewish … what do they think? When I came to believe in Yeshua, my DNA changed? Someone exchanged my blood for Gentile blood?"

Her body still facing the passenger door, she pleaded, "Daniel, he didn't mean it …" She hurriedly pivoted her body to now face him. "He was so nice, just maybe ignorant about, you know, people like us."

"People like us—and exactly what are we now? Let me ask you something, Naomi. Do you think Yeshua would want us to stay Jewish?"

"I don't know."

"I *do* know—God does not want us to say we converted. Naomi, I believe that if we continue saying we are Jewish, that honors Him."

"But, Daniel, think about the good ... I mean you could teach Hebrew at their church ... and what do you think about going to Bible College? I got goosebumps when Ray mentioned that."

Those pleading eyes of hers, how could he want to do anything but make her happy? Daniel turned off the motor, pulled the key from the ignition and placed his hand on Naomi's lap. "Let's talk about this after we get into the house." His hand went down to her knee and squeezed it in that special way which always made her jump and then giggle. "I gotta go to the bathroom."

"Me, too. Which one you want?"

"The guest one," Naomi answered. "It's closer."

"Good, I get ours."

Since it seemed there was now a pressing need, she didn't wait for him to open her car door but instead walked out on her own. Once inside, Naomi noticed the blinking red light on their answering machine—it was always the first thing she checked when entering the house, a holdover from the days when she anxiously waited to hear if she "got the part." She quickly hit the play button on the machine.

"Hello, I'm Sam Needleman. I'm with Apple of God's Eye Ministry. I read about you in the Sun-Sentinel and we need to talk. Call me at 312-597-9432."

JUNE 1980

Weekends were the hardest. The Village Voice crumpled up on the floor where she had flung it. The singles events all cost too much money and the personals all sounded like losers looking for winners. All she had to look forward to was Monday and going back to her office job.

Fun—not! She could have had a job as a waitress—that's what a lot of the members of her acting class did—one even told her a café to go and visit, that they were looking for help. But, no, Dad adamantly said, "No one in our family ever slung hash. It's not going to start now."

And only Dad could come up with this dumb Martha Washington Hotel for Women. "I want you to be safe." So what if the bathroom was down the hall, to be shared with like twenty others. She shuffled the cards as Dad had taught her, spread the cards across the narrow twin bed, and then began the umpteenth game of solitaire. She always won—she always cheated.

It's not like aloneness was something new to her. Aloneness, she guessed, was her lot in life. Better get used to it. A room with no doors—was this her destiny? No! Succeeding in theatre would be her destiny. Fame and a big "I told you so" to all those who had rejected her—that was her destiny.

Also in that month, a rabbinical student named Daniel Cantor was having lunch at his Aunt Luba's home in Brooklyn. Aunt Luba with her beautiful blonde hair and blue eyes. Ever since meeting this exotic lovely woman at his family's Passover Seder, he treasured spending time with her.

Aunt Luba had already stuffed him with her stuffed cabbage and now was bringing out the pastries—a whole tray-full. "Did I ever tell you, my *boychik*, the only reason I was alive and at your *bris* was because your aunt was graced with looking like a *shiksa*. Papa, my dear Papa, before they took him away, he told me, my *Lubala*, *loyfn fest*, run fast. You look like one of them, but never forget, my daughter, you are a *Yid*.

All the many times Daniel was told this story by his beautiful aunt, each time it just increased his love for this woman.

"*Esen*. Eat. I know you think of your mother—if only she looked like me—but God looked out for her—and your father, too. Now I have my little *boychik*. The rest of our family … they are no more. But you, *oy*, I'm so proud, a rabbi no less!

Tapping his fingers on their dining room table, Daniel tried to wait patiently for his wife. She always took longer in the bathroom than him. Normally that was okay, but today two things were making him anxious. There was the uncommon tension between them and, secondly, there was this question of who was this Sam? Five more minutes if no appearance by Naomi, he'd call by himself—but that was not the way they did things. Always it was together—at least for momentous moments.

The first thing she saw when she opened the door was her husband doing the drumming his fingers thing. *Uh oh.* It wasn't her imagination then, this tension between them. She took a beat then tried to sound casual. "Wow, a big burger, French fries, and a shake—never saw you that hungry before—at least I don't think I have."

Her smile was weak but it communicated an olive branch and he gladly accepted it. "And you, you ate like a bird—except for that cherry pit."

With a startled laugh, she asked, "You saw that?"

"Thought we'd have to take you to the dentist."

With the tension dissolved, she asked, "Did you want to call this Sam person?"

FEBRUARY 1981

Rocking with the rude sway of the subway, brakes squealing, all her life having felt alone, why at this time did she feel more unwanted than ever before? A culmination to all her days on earth. Simply defining who she was. Would any of these strangers, their heads buried in their newspaper, even notice the tears flooding her face?

A flash of memory. About ten years old, with Dad in a department store, a mirror—with a momentary reflection—hurled Naomi into what she knew was reality. *I'll never be one of the pretty ones.* And now today, she chose to reject this thing growing inside her. Gary doesn't want it—then she will discard it just like she's been discarded. It all began and ended in the knowledge that Gary simply didn't want her.

The rocking motion from the subway could actually be therapeutic if she let it. Like a basic primal instinct, once rocked by our mothers, somehow we revert to rocking ourselves, desperately and unconsciously working to soothe ourselves. But today she was doing what no decent mother would or should do. *Well, that's okay, I'm choosing not to be a mother—I can't be one. I don't want to be one.*

The address Gary gave her squeezed so intensely in her hand that the ink was almost too blurry to read. Didn't matter, she had memorized the address. Gary only repeated it like five times, asking her to repeat it back to him. He even said he'd send her some money to help once the Hollywood bigshots gave him an advance on his blockbuster idea. Then he'd be back. But no baby would. Once gone, never ever would "it" come back. But, of course, that was the idea.

But would Gary ever come back? She knew he wouldn't. *How much more will I mess up my life looking for someone to tell me I'm pretty? Naomi, you never will. Stop looking.*

Having changed to a comfortable pair of khaki Dockers and a white Polo shirt, Daniel found Naomi still primping in front of the mirror. "Honey, we need to leave and meet him at the airport in about an hour. Whatever you wear, you look pretty. But especially the navy pantsuit. I love that on you."

When they had called the number from the message, Sam's office picked up and explained Sam was on his way to Palm Beach. When Daniel explained who he was, the secretary explained, "Oh, Rabbi Needleman was hoping to meet with you when he arrived. His parents live in West Palm, but while vising them he was hoping to meet with you."

"What is Apple of God's Eye?"

"Oh, Rabbi Cantor, the ministry's whole purpose is to tell Jewish people about their Messiah. If you can still meet him, I can give you his flight number and arrival time. I can also have him paged at O'Hare and let him know you'll be there in Florida to meet him."

Chapter Six

Us Against Them?

"Flight 407 from Chicago now arriving at Gate Eight."

"Daniel, how will we know which one is him?"

"Honey, relax. He saw our picture in the newspaper—he'll recognize us."

Boom! A short, dark-haired bearded man wearing a well-fitting suit was walking toward them. He was also wearing a blue velvet yarmulke. *Wait! I thought he was a Christian, like us.* The man was holding Sun Sentinel's Sunday edition, pointing to their photo. "Found you!"

Broadly smiling, he pumped Daniel's hand. Naomi assumed eventually he would look and acknowledge her. With a short distance between them, she tried not coughing from the fumes of his strongly-scented aftershave. She was also keenly aware that the Rabbi's suit was a very expensive one—silk most likely, she thought. Having a father who was in the "cloak and suit trade," she had learned a thing or two. And there was the man she adored, in the comfy dockers he had worn when she first met him—and still with his beat-up loafers, same ones from that first meeting as well, and, yes, still without socks.

She had been basking in the memory of her first encounter with Daniel when she heard Sam's voice, his hand extended toward her. With her best theatrical smile, she greeted him and asked his and Daniel's pardon. "I'm sorry, but I need the ladies' room. See you in a minute."

With the tilt of his head and a furrowed brow, Daniel gave her his "what's going on?" face. She shrugged her shoulders and smiled, understanding why he was concerned. It really was not that she wanted to run from this Christian rabbi, or whatever you'd want to call him—it was simply she seemed to be excusing herself a bit more often lately for a trip to the bathroom. She knew what she hoped it could indicate but dared not even entertain such an idea.

When Naomi returned, she saw the two men engaged in a lively conversation—as if they were old friends. For a moment she thought the queasiness that had brought her to the bathroom was returning. While hesitating by the ladies' room sign, Daniel hurriedly walked to her.

"Honey, we are going to go to your favorite deli in West Palm. Sam's treating us for lunch."

A free meal—was that why he was grinning ear to ear?

Pulling out Naomi's chair for her, Daniel said, "You know what I found out? Sam's parents believe in Yeshua, too."

"Really?" She turned to Sam and asked, "You mean you grew up—?"

Sam's smile broadened as he scraped a few burnt areas from his bagel. "*Ken!* You do know Hebrew, don't you? I assumed—"

Daniel nodded and answered, "*Ken!*"

Sam nodded. "I'm one of the rare breeds, I must say—blessed to be raised in a Messianic home. *Baruch Hashem[1].* My parents were the ones to begin Apple of God's Eye. It started as a Bible study when my sister and I were in our teens. Suddenly there were people coming over to our house—it took a lot of getting used to. My sister resented it and I was too busy with baseball to care. We were in Jersey then and years later, after I went through intense study, I

---

1   Thank God

moved to Chicago and continued my parents' work there. I'm sorry to say my sister still is resentful. In other words, she doesn't believe."

Naomi picked up her bagel. The plentiful supply of cream cheese oozed out and almost plopped onto her linen pants. Wanting to learn as much as she could as quickly as she could, she placed her bagel back on the plate. "I didn't know there was any such ... I don't know what to call ... well, your secretary used the word ministry on the phone."

Sam snickered. "I understand, you think they have the corner on our Messiah. The Gentiles and their churches."

Naomi pursed her lips but Daniel responded immediately, "Yes, I was afraid it was like that."

Sam leaned across the table, looking intently at Daniel. "Rabbi, I am glad I got to you before *they* did. Before you know it, they'll be calling you converted—saying something like 'when you were Jewish.'"

Daniel nodded and Sam dropped his fork. "Aha, I can tell by your expression, they already said that garbage to you, haven't they?"

Naomi in a voice meant only for Daniel, said, "I'm sure Ray didn't mean to ... well, you know, I mean he's a nice man."

Sam chuckled and asked Daniel, "Would you mind if I speak to your wife?"

Daniel turned to Naomi. "Is it okay with you, spouse?"

Naomi, her lips still pursed, turned to Sam and asked, "Yes?"

"Mrs. Cantor, I believe we need to make sure we get off on the right foot, don't you?"

She nodded.

"The other day my parents called and read the interview you both had with the newspaper. In it, you said something about having a personal problem and that you called a support group—and they are the ones who told you about our Messiah. Do I have that right?"

"Yes, that is correct."

"I'm not trying to meddle, please believe me, but assuming this was a Christian group, you must be very grateful to them." He placed the palm of his hand over his heart and lowered his head. "And here I am, to your ears anyway, tearing apart these people."

"You are correct again," she said.

Sam looked toward Daniel for a quick second, laughed, and shook his head. "Don't you just love our women? Jewish women—heaven forbid a *goy* try and manage them—only us Jews can deal with them."

Naomi spoke in a staccato voice. "Please don't use the word, *goy*." She thrust her chin forward and asked, "I mean, are you okay if someone calls us a *kike*?"

"Whoa," both Daniel and Sam exclaimed.

Daniel hugged Naomi and kissed the top of her forehead. "My beautiful wife—I adore her."

"Yes," Sam agreed, "together you will be a wonderful ministry team. People will love the both of you." Sam swallowed his coffee, placed the cup down, and smiled. "I know I'm hitting you both with a lot right away, and it's all so new to you. Let me explain—actually, it will explain two things at once. First off, *goys*—excuse me, Gentiles, have been known to say some derogatory things about us as well. For example, when I speak at one of their churches—maybe doing a Passover Seder—"

Daniel's eyebrows lifted. "You do Seders at churches?"

"Oh, Rabbi, you have so much to learn. But presentations like that will be an opportunity for both of you to be a team—usually it's just one of us men, but these churches will love having a couple. And as for the things some of them say, get this one—I'm at a book table, you know selling some of our books, some cassette tapes, a magazine we publish—oh yes, we publish a magazine—and a *goy*—excuse me, Mrs. Cantor, a Gentile, comes up to me, asks how much one of the items is and I tell him '$9.95.' He laughs and says, 'isn't that just like you Jews—not $10 but $9.95.' Tell me, Mrs. Cantor, do you find that remark offensive?"

"Yes of course."

"But that's the way they think. And if you're not careful, they'll get you thinking you're not a Jew anymore." Wagging his fork at the couple, he warned, "Listen to me, you are still Jewish—and the more you don't forget it, the more God can use you." Sam held up his small glass of orange juice, put it to his lips, but then paused and gave his full attention to Daniel "I saw your expression when I called you 'Rabbi' a minute ago. You don't think you should be called that anymore, do you?"

Daniel reached down and squeezed Naomi's knee while staring at Sam. "How'd you know?"

"Listen to me, Rabbi Cantor, you are *still* a rabbi. But now you are a special one. Have you ever heard of a messianic rabbi?"

Daniel placed his hands on his chin with his eyes widening, he shook his head.

"They might tell you you're a Christian,--that you converted … whatever, but listen to me. You have found your Messiah, right? So you, me, your wife, and my family, we are messianic Jews—and messianic Jews need a rabbi, don't they?"

When Naomi saw Daniel's face light up, she knew voicing concern would not be a good idea. *What about Ray and Melinda? I guess Sam would call them "those people"—kinda like us against them.*

Daniel responded, "How does one become a messianic rabbi?"

"Apple of God's Eye will send you to the best Bible institute in the country—it's in Chicago. If you sign a covenant with us, or what you might call a contract, we will pay your tuition, as well as providing room and board for both you and your wife."

Daniel turned to Naomi. "Do you believe this?"

Rather than responding to Daniel's question, she slowly lifted her bagel from the plate and used her tongue to slowly lick the excess cream cheese spilling out from the sides of the bagel.

Daniel stared at her for a few moments, and then finally asked, "Naomi?"

With both men's eyes studying her, she nonchalantly sipped her water. Her parents paid a lot of money for her acting classe many years ago and so why not try to utilize all she learned? She placed her hand on Daniel's knee and asked Sam, "With this covenant, what are we agreeing to?"

Sam smiled at Daniel. "Nothing like a Jewish wife—smart, huh?" Looking directly at Naomi, he explained, "Your husband will be agreeing to work for our ministry for at least four years after he finishes at the Institute."

"What kind of work will I be doing?" Daniel asked.

"Simple. You'll be a messianic rabbi. Once you've graduated from the institute, we will send you back to Florida. With all the Jewish people here but no Messianic ministry nearby, it's a shame. But you, Rabbi, you are God's answer to our prayers. We'll help you start a messianic synagogue. The Bible institute's semester will begin in September, so we have at most two months to get you registered and set everything up."

"We have a house in Boca we will need to sell," Naomi protested. "And a pastor at a church we visited already made a similar offer."

The pupils of Sam's eyes constricted as he turned to Daniel. Sam tapped a finger on the table. "Rabbi, let me explain something to you. The g—gentiles in the church, they will use you as a trophy. They'll put you on display." He laughed, put his hand on his chest, and leaned across the table toward Daniel. "Let Apple of God's Eye use you instead. And as for your house," he smiled at Naomi, "according to the reporter in your interview, it's some house. Well, I have an idea how you can keep it."

Naomi wished she could have kept her mouth shut, but instead she exclaimed, "Really? How?"

"I'll have to check with my father, but I know Dad's been restless and talked about making an attempt to plant a new messianic congregation in your area. What if you let my Dad—maybe Mom, too—live in your beautiful home in Boca. No need to worry, Mrs. Cantor—my mom is your typical Jewish lady—she'll have your house even cleaner than you have it right now. So, not only do they live in your home, keeping it ready for you to move back into—and the ministry giving you money for rent, but here's the 'not only that' part of it—Dad will start building a congregation for you to lead when you get back in Boca." Sam rubbed his fingers on the lapel of his suit jacket and announced, "Brilliant idea, if I do say so myself."

Naomi couldn't help herself when she breathed out a "wow."

Sam continued, "And when in Chicago, Mrs. Cantor, you can work for me—as a secretary. That will at least give you both some spending money. And, Rabbi, you will have some first-hand experience in Chicago as well. You see, I have a congregation in the suburbs of Chicago, and you will have a hand in helping run the services. That'll give you a taste of what you'll be doing in Boca." Sam snapped his fingers together, "Oh, I should have asked—the newspaper article didn't mention children—does this mean you have no children—at least as of yet?"

Daniel jumped in, "Yes, at least for now."

When their waitress brought the check, she started to give it to Daniel, but Sam quickly snatched it. He took out a plastic card from his wallet and explained, "This will be a ministry expense. Oh, another thing—I'm telling you, the ideas are just popping out of my head. Mrs. Cantor, the article mentioned you were an actress at one time."

Naomi nodded.

"Do you sing? And dance?"

"Yes."

"Well, your talent will be put to good use, I can assure you." Sam pulled his chair back and stood. "My parents are going to be anxiously waiting for me."

And at that moment, in walked a couple. The man was wearing fringe hanging down from his shirt and his wife's hair was hidden under a drab scarf. The orthodox Jewish man's yarmulke appeared almost the same as Sam's. They were accompanied by four toddlers and a baby in a stroller. More to contemplate. Were they simply orthodox or perhaps they were messianic, too. How could she know?

FEBRUARY 1981

On that same cold February day, several hours after the deed was done, again she was rocked by the sway of the rude subway tracks. She had expected something that would bear at least a slight resemblance to a medical facility—out of courtesy at least. However, instead she found herself walking into a nondescript gray building—no sign, nothing. The staff didn't seem to care what it looked like. Why should they bother? Every woman from the lobby to the elevator, and into the waiting room, kept their faces masked. None wanted to see or be seen.

In the waiting room, there was this one older-looking woman who had a male companion with her. He was holding her hand. Naomi hated this woman—she hated the man with her—she hated Gary—she hated herself.

But what she had done wasn't all her fault. Gary had taken for granted she didn't want this child—this bother—this impediment to their career—*BUT NO, IT WAS MY FAULT. I never once told him, "I want this baby."* For she knew the devastating rejection she would feel as Gary would probably just hang up on her. But maybe one day maybe Gary will marry her and they'll have another child and they'd still have their glorious careers. *Maybe I don't deserve anything that good.*

Tossed about by the train, her mind tried to run from the whole event. That crazy doctor, how dare him? Jewish himself and asking her before starting the procedure, "So, are you religious?" How dare him. What? It wasn't like *Yom Kippur* or anything.

Riding home after meeting with Sam Needleman, Naomi tried to escape from this sense of dread. She had been pushed into doing the unspeakable with Gary—and now cursed with being childless, she must not fear rejection again, but this time use her voice—and her mind—and her intuition, too. "Daniel, I know you like Sam's offer, but what if we just asked Ray what he thought about it."

"Why should we do that?"

With the uncharacteristic sharpness of his response, Naomi retreated. "It was just a suggestion. No big deal."

Daniel actually never heard Naomi's question. It had only been a momentary distraction as he had been recalling another day spent with his Aunt Luba.

He was sitting with his aunt on that heavily-worn couch—the memory so vivid, he could feel the prickling from the upholstery. A large scrapbook was wide open, spread out between her lap and Daniel's.

A teardrop falling onto the sepia crinkled photo, as she told him, "This was the family— saved me from dying—*gut* people. Christian people. Half their food they give to me. But never forget sweet *boychik*, we are *Yids*."

"Did they try to force you to convert?"

"No, God forbid, Danieleh. They knew Luba is a *Yid*. Their religion *gut*—they pray sweet but not for us. One night bad dream. I on big, very big, mountain, but I see bigger mountain, prettier than my mountain, flowers, even birds, singing *tweet tweet*. I'm oh so jealous—I want pretty mountain for me. You know what happen then? I wake up!"

Daniel loved teasing his vivacious aunt. "It's *gut*, otherwise you'd fall and die."

Wagging a finger at him, she scolded. "Just like your mother—your sister always played tricks on me. Zofia tease, now you tease. Ah! My young sister's boy, he make me proud. If I could have had … never mind, I couldn't. Your mother, she live through camps, God give her good son. A rabbi now! Convert? *Oy, a shkandal!²* I tell you secret—this Christian family put wooden cross with man nailed on it right by my bed. That's why bad dream. Our Torah, my sweet boy, is full of wonderful old men with white beards—and our *shuls*, when young I loved watching Papa drinking schnapps with all the men—all of them dancing with the Torah. I can see them—holding scroll like it was their baby. Convert?" With a soft guttural sound, she scoffed at the thought.

---

2   Oh, what a scandal!

Chapter Seven

Who's Tamar?

"Too Jewish—what?" He will never understand this woman. When he had asked her why she wasn't excited about Sam's offer—"a God-given opportunity, Naomi," all he got was a few mumbles and then some stutters, until finally she blurted out, "Too Jewish!"

Finally they were able to create a détente—the next morning each would write their own list of pros and cons. "Lord willing," Daniel said as they retired for the night, "we will come to an agreement."

He stayed awake through most of the night, coming up with the obvious pros—and the only con being Naomi's wacky stubbornness. Too Jewish? With the first sighting of morning light, he quietly rolled out of bed assuming it would be like most mornings when Naomi would sleep a good hour after he had gotten up. However, on this particular morning, he awoke even earlier than usual eager to write down all his pros, but Naomi's side of the bed was empty.

Then he heard her in the guest bathroom making horrible gagging sounds.

Thirty minutes later, Naomi had gotten her land legs back and ventured into the kitchen. Was it applesauce they say is good? Or is it crackers? Before she could make a decision, she heard the front door open. Quickly grabbing a kitchen knife, she carefully stuck her head out to see who was coming in, only to see Daniel breeze in holding a small shopping bag from Walgreens.

"I thought you were still in bed," she gasped while walking toward him.

"Naomi, could you put the knife down, honey? I'm sorry I scared you." He reached into the bag and produced a home pregnancy test.

"But, but …"

"I've seen the signs, honey. Please it's time to check."

The tears fell. "I've tried too many times. I can't … I can't … not again. I don't want to be disappointed again."

Simply holding her hands tightly and his face fully acknowledging her pain, her "no" became an "all right, I'll try." She took the test to the bathroom and locked the door. Daniel prayed—and grabbed himself some much-needed coffee as well as Naomi's *God's Promises* book. Opening to her bookmark, he found a verse she had highlighted:

Delight yourself in the Lord and He will give you the desires of your heart. Psalm 37:4

Soon Naomi was standing before him, beaming. In the middle of a joyful embrace, she abruptly pulled away. "But we're unemployed. A broke pregnant couple."

Before Daniel could process this sobering realization, Naomi broke in. "Let's go with Sam. Sam Needleman."

"Are you sure? Honey, don't—"

"Please, Daniel, call him right away. And tell him I'm pregnant—ask him if that's okay."

They shortly heard Sam exclaim *"mazel tov³."* Everything was fine—they would now be the newest recruits to Apple of God's Eye ministry.

Thus, began the intense rush to have Daniel registered with Moody Bible Institute and arrange for housing in Chicago. Sam's mother, Lillian, was very warm and friendly, which helped Naomi brush away any remnants of her past misgivings—*I am Jewish so how could anything be too Jewish?*

---

3   Hebrew phrase expressing congratulations

It was an overwhelming task deciding what to pack and take with them and what to leave behind. Since Daniel's time was largely taken up sitting under Sam's tutelage, the sorting and packing pretty much were left to Naomi.

All the kitchen things, Naomi thought, could be used by the Needleman's whenever they chose to stay in Boca. Then, of course, there was the enormous relief that they would be returning in a few years, with supposedly a congregation up and running for Daniel to lead.

Lillian was an immense help. She and her husband Howie had quite a bit of experience with moving from city to city, setting up these messianic congregations. "I lose count, sweetheart. Howie and I, as I remember it, moved from New Jersey to Philadelphia, then from there to Los Angeles, and maybe then Phoenix, I think. Oh well, at some point we ended up here in Florida. But don't worry, dear, Howie and I will take good care of your home til you get back. And when you do, you'll get to be a rabbi's wife all over again."

And it wasn't until Lillian asked what obstetrician she was using, that Naomi realized they had forgotten a very important item for their to-do list. Although Lillian offered to ask her friends who they'd recommend, Naomi chose instead to ask Melinda. Without hesitation, Melinda gave her the phone number and address for Dr. Romero.

The night before Naomi's appointment with the doctor, the reality stunned her. She would be carrying a baby all the way until delivery. Basking in God's presence, she finally believed that she had been forgiven. And now a new life would come into this world. Her hands lovingly cradled her stomach. The exquisite wonder. Hers and Daniel's bodies together had formed a new life. A life that was half him and half her. This new life united them for eternity. Two separate human beings, once strangers, now inextricably linked. Never would they be parted. Being made one flesh—such new resonating splendor. She thanked and praised Jesus for this miraculous system He had ordained, where new life was produced by the love of two who had eternally committed their lives to one another. Now their love was multiplied forever by the beginnings of a new life being knit together inside her.

Lying flat on the hard metal examination table, Naomi stared at the blue acoustic ceiling tiles. Their edges were frayed and other areas showed fading blotches. How old was Dr. Romero's office? Well, if Melinda recommended him, he must be good.

The heavy wooden door opened. "Hello, Mrs. Cantor. My name is Stephanie. I'll be your technician for today." The young petite blonde smiled as she opened a tube and then squirted some bluish gel onto Naomi's abdomen. Naomi flinched at the unexpected coldness.

"Sorry, I know it's cold," Stephanie said softly. "This stuff helps the sound waves travel." Stephanie leaned her face into Naomi's. "You look nervous, but it'll be over in a few minutes. It helps the doctor see how your baby is doing."

When Naomi saw the technician pick up a small wand, she sat up and asked, "What's that?"

"Please lay back down. It's going to be fine." She held the wand in front of Naomi's eyes and explained, "This is called a transducer. It's going to help us see images of your baby. I need you to hold your breath for a little while, okay?"

Such a strange sensation, feeling this metal-type thing sliding around her belly and wondering what were the images. "You don't deserve a baby—you killed your first one—maybe this one will be—." She hoped the girl standing over her didn't notice the tears gliding down her cheek. The only way to shut out the accusing voice was to pray, which Naomi did just as Melinda had taught her. *Thank you, Yeshua, for You have forgiven me.* Then she heard a sudden gasp.

Stephanie stepped away from the table, put down her wand, and explained, "I need to get Dr. Romero. You wait there—and just relax." The door halfway open, she turned back to tell Naomi, "You can breathe now."

Eternity passed as she waited for the doctor. When Dr. Romero entered the room, Naomi bolted upright. "What's the matter with my baby?"

Taking off his glasses, Dr. Romero approached Naomi and placed a hand on her shoulder. "Mrs. Cantor, there is nothing wrong with either of your babies."

That evening, Daniel and Naomi called to deliver the good news to Naomi's parents. Saul Goldblatt, when learning his daughter would be having twins, told her, "Good. Now one of them can be a Jew like you used to be, and the other one can go be a Gentile."

Helen Goldblatt thankfully had a very different reaction. She was ecstatic and made a small request. "Sweetheart, would you do something for me? If one of your twins is a girl, would you name her Tamar?"

"Tamar? Who's Tamar, Mom?"

Seeing Daniel's quizzical look, Naomi shrugged her shoulders. "Mom, who's Tamar?"

Chapter Eight

23 Years Later
June 2011
Tallahassee,
Florida

"Wait—your last name is Cantor ... from Boca? Tamara squeezed her linen napkin tightly and tucked her chin into her chest. "Yes, Mr. Steinberg," she murmured.

"And your father is a rabbi?"

Tamara nodded.

"*Daniel* Cantor? Is Rabbi Daniel Cantor your father?"

"Yes."

He stood and leaned over the table towering over Tamara. The volume of his voice increased with each word and his face turned a dangerous red. She pushed her seat back. Across the large table, Jesse just sat. Tamara opened her hands and tipped her head forward to invite her boyfriend's intervention. His eyes widened as he mouthed "What?"

Mr. Steinberg explained to his son, "I read about her father years ago—he's a traitor." Turning back to Tamara, he clenched his jaw and sharply pointed his finger at her then toward the front door. "Get out of my house now."

Back to Jesse, he said. "You are not to see this girl again. Do you hear me?" He forcefully sat down as if to punctuate his command.

Tamara stood, looked across the table for help, but instead Jesse's head was bowed.

"Where is my purse, Mrs. Steinberg?"

"What dear? You're speaking so low I can't hear you. "

"Never mind. I remember where it was."

Halfway out of the dining room, she paused and turned once again toward Jesse. Was he ever going to say anything?

"Get out now and stay away from my son."

She found her shoulder bag in the parlor hanging from a chair. Hands shaking, she slung it over her shoulder and at the front door, she turned back once again. No, he was not coming. Her dirty red Camaro was all that offered refuge.

My parents were right. I should have left as soon as I graduated.

That had been her plan too, until she met Jesse. Screenwriting 101—there he sat with his curly hair and snarky smile. She immediately disliked him—she recognized smugness when she saw it. Yet this smugness became endearing when he sat next to her in the snack bar and turned in her direction. All her defenses came down when he told her, "Whenever I produce a film, whatever it's about, you have to be the star of it."

"And how are you going to produce your own film? Like who do you know? Do you know someone with money?"

"Yeah," he said as that oh-so-cute conceited smile returned. "My dad. He's got mega bucks."

But now, this self-assured future producer had cowered to Mr. Megabucks. Her potential first real boyfriend snatched away from her. Hands trembling, she started the car. Were it not a ritzy neighborhood she would have peeled out. Yet this gave her time to drive slowly and look at her Blackberry. A voicemail. She couldn't deal with it. She needed a cigarette. Tamara reached into her purse, pulled out her pack. One left.

Half an hour later, needing another cigarette, she quickly pulled off of I-90 and made a sharp turn into a drugstore parking lot where she came to a screeching halt.

Time to listen to the voicemail.

Mom. "Honey, we miss you so much. Why won't you at least call us? Dad and I are praying for you. Please call—or even more, come home."

Tamara hit delete and opened her wallet. Enough to buy another pack. She threw the phone into her bag but retrieved it when it pinged. A text. Jesse.

"What did your Dad do? Mine won't even tell me. But, baby, I miss you. Let's meet tomorrow for breakfast."

She tapped out "k" and added a big red heart. Time to buy a pack—and if he texts back great, but I'm going into the store.

A few minutes later, an unopened pack in one hand and a five-dollar bill in the other, Tamara's phone rang. "Wait a minute, please," she asked the cashier and dug into her pocketbook. The face on the screen was not Jesse's.

"Hey, Zac, I'm in a store. Let me call you back when I get in the car."

She thanked the clerk and returned to her car. She left her car door open while lighting up—Jesse always complained about the smell of stale cigarettes in her car. Guess she won't have to worry about that anymore. She hit redial.

"Hey, Zac."

"Hey, princess. I've missed you."

"Really?"

"Don't sound so shocked. We all miss—"

"Please, don't go there—that's all I hear from each of you—when are you coming home and stuff. I'm tired of being treated like the prodigal daughter."

"Sorry, Sis, but you are." Zac hesitated. "You're smoking, aren't you?"

"What? How'd—"

"Just twin-tuition."

Tamara threw her cigarette to the ground and stomped it out with her shoe. With a gulp, she admitted, "I miss you, too."

"Hey, Tammy, could you say that a little louder? I'm not sure—"

"Stop it. You know I hate being called Tammy!"

She heard him clear his throat. "Tamara, will you tell me what's going on with you?"

She bit her lip and fought back sobbing. The sound of her brother's voice was like being home for her. "Isaac, the truth is I don't know."

"Oh, we're using proper names now? Tamara, that's cold."

"Zac, it's anything but cold. I'm sorry—it was just a stupid way to come back at you. I'm stupid like that." She knew him—he would jump to her defense if she gave him an opening, so she quickly continued. "Ever since graduation, I've had all this anger. I don't fit in—anywhere."

"Dad said you're dating some guy you met at a synagogue? So, do you think you fit in more there than at Dad's congregation?"

"It's not that simple. I wish I could—"

"Come home and we can talk about it, okay? My show is coming up in about ten minutes. Can you tune it in—I'll play a song dedicated to you, okay?"

She bit her lip again. "Okay. I will. Thanks."

"98.6, just in case you forgot. Oh, and before you hang up, I need to tell you something. It's actually the reason I called. Grandma Helen isn't doing well."

"What? What's wrong with *Bubbe*?"

"Breast cancer."

"No. If I come home, can I see her?"

"Of course. You know that would bless her. I think she loves you more than anyone."

After saying goodbye to her brother, she sat, smoked, and stared into space Tamara had nowhere to go. Her apartment had become even more depressing now that her organic-eating, earth-shoe-wearing roommate moved to California. Why go home? Just to sit in front of the TV screen or stare at her phone hoping for Jesse to call? No way.

Why not stare at a movie screen instead?

She wasn't all that far from the Cinema. Friday date night. All those couples—oh well, she could hide her pathetic life in the back.

From a short distance away, she was able to read the marquee. The choices were Chronicles of Narnia (no way—I remember Dad reading that to me as a kid), Kingdom of Heaven (no way, enough religion already), and Ice Princess (why not, that's what Jesse calls me). Unable to read the show times, she shrugged her shoulders. Who says you have to begin at the beginning?

It was time to hear Zac and hear what song he would play for her. After a short commercial break, she heard his voice. "This song is dedicated to my twin sister. Tamara, I hope you are listening."

Come home, come home. You who are weary come home …

Enough. She grabbed her pocketbook and heard the muffled sound of her phone. She grabbed it quickly, but before she could see if it was Jesse calling, the shiny metal object slipped from her hand and fell somewhere between the driver's seat and the console. She wiggled her hand in the narrow opening to retrieve the phone. It was impossible. What if her hand got stuck?

The sound of the incessant ringtone was torture. She squinted into the crack where the phone was wedged. Using every possible angle, she still was not able to identify the caller.

"I give up," Tamara said to no one. She shook her head, shrugged her shoulders, and slammed the car door. The sight of all the couples waiting in line stopped her. Maybe it was Jesse calling. She ran back to the car and tried dislodging the driver's seat from its tracks. No amount of yanking would work. Another approach was called for—I mean what if it were Jesse who called? From the back seat of her car, she was better able to reach it. With the tail end of a comb, she managed to coax it out.

She tapped voicemail. "Hello Ms. Cantor, this is Arthur Seagram with Human Resources. We regret to tell you that as of now we cannot consider your application for news reporter with WTWC. We appreciate the administrative work you have done for us, and perhaps with time—."

Delete.

If only she could delete this whole day. Rejection, rejection, rejection, with a little breast cancer on top. How much could she take? She should just run away. If she left tomorrow to see *Bubbe* she'd probably have to call the station to let them know she wasn't coming in on Monday—and maybe they'd think it was her being a sore loser—but who cares. They don't think well of her anyway.

Forget the movie—she needed Grandma Helen. She picked up a frozen pizza and a pint of Ben & Jerry's Brownie Batter ice cream. Tamara's Big Friday Night Date—pig out and play video games. She wished she could see her *Bubbe* and cry on her shoulder.

A few games later, with scraps of crust sitting on her plate and half a container of ice cream melting on her coffee table, Tamara stared into space. Her dreams were smashed. No on-camera TV reporting and no boyfriend. And with the loss of the boyfriend, no dream about producing and acting in a movie—that was probably a pie-in-the-sky thing anyway.

Her family would tell her, "Tamara, you need to trust in God. Have faith. God has a plan for you and He works all things together for good." And, of course, they would have scolded her for dating Jesse anyway. "How could you—he's not a believer."

Family. She forgot she was going to call, but it was too late now. *Bubbe* went to bed probably by nine o'clock. She picked up the dirty plate and the mushy paper container with brown soup oozing out.

It was a fitful night's sleep. At the first glimpse of light, she trudged out of bed, made coffee, and sat on her terrace, recalling one of her most treasured memories with *Bubbe.*

Her sweet sixteen party. The traditional song had been sung. Birthday candles blown out. And no one had noticed Tamara was no longer with them. At least she thought no one noticed. Alone in the family room, she held up her new Jewish star necklace to the dimming sunlight. Prisms of red, yellow, and indigo dancing across the walls from the triangles of glass, each piece of the star a different vibrant color. No matter what her classmates said, she was still a Jew. She tried to ignore the gentle tapping at the door.

"Tamaleh, can I come in?"

"*Bubbe.*" She jumped up and welcomed her. "I love your present. Would you help me put it on?" Tamara placed it in *Bubbe's* hands and turned away and lifted her long red hair off her shoulders. Once the necklace had been placed around her neck, Tamara took *Bubbe's* hand. "Come, let's sit on the couch."

"Is the star—the necklace—is it okay?"

"Of course, *Bubbe.* I love it. Why wouldn't it be okay?"

"It's so confusing—your mother and father's religion. I don't want …"

"I wouldn't worry. You know, Mom gets upset about lots of things. At least with me she does. *Bubbe,* how are you doing? Granddad's been gone now almost a year. I'm sorry, I should visit you more."

"You have your own life. But soon, you'll be driving. You can come and take me to the beach. *Nu?*" Just the shortest time of awkward silence before Helen leaned into Tamara. "What's bothering you, would you tell me?"

How could she tell her grandmother? Tamara's parents were always talking about how Helen needed to be saved. She needed what they had. Jesus. Joy. Peace. So, how could she let on to her *Bubbe* that she felt no joy, no peace—and can't say Jesus, gotta say Yeshua, so actually no Jesus. Gotta win her to the Lord, that's what they always said—and even Zac, he joined in on that pious look of worry—Helen would be left not going to heaven unless they could save her.

But how could she not answer *Bubbe*? She was sitting there looking so uncomfortable. Probably afraid she had asked Tamara a question she shouldn't have, so when she began to rise from the couch, Tamara took her hand and asked her to stay. "Please."

Helen did stay and continued holding her Tamaleh's hand as she spoke. "I guess maybe sometimes you might feel like a stranger with us. I mean we're not Jewish, but yet we do all these Jewish things, and I guess maybe we are Jewish. Yeah, of course, we are Jewish, but not to most everyone. Right?"

"I don't want to upset your mother. I don't understand your religion, but that's not my business."

"Forget that stuff. I just want to ask you, *Bubbe*, when you were my age, did you have a boyfriend?"

"Oh, sugar, you ask good questions."

"*Bubbe*, you're blushing!"

"My sisters had boyfriends all through school, but not me. They said I was too serious. But eventually Moishe Kermish?"

Tamara exclaimed, "Moishe Kermish?"

"He was Hersh Siegel's cousin, from Mobile."

"I'm sorry for laughing—it's just those names."

"Good thing I met Saul Goldblatt, isn't it? And you know your mother changed her name to Gold before she married your father."

"Yeah, I know, her stage name. Mom says she named me Tamara because you asked her to. Who was Tamara?"

"Do you like your name?" Glad to receive a nod, Helen explained, "You are named after Tamar—but, sweetheart, I can't talk about her."

"Huh?"

"You know, every family has a skeleton in its closet. I found a photograph one day in my mother's jewelry box. I showed my mother the picture and she snatched it out of my hand. Told me,

'You must never talk about this woman.' So I never did, but that photograph, I just couldn't stop thinking about it. Seeing it in my sleep." She pinched her granddaughter's cheek. "And here you are, my sweet Tamara."

Now here she was, six years later, still without a boyfriend. *Stop feeling sorry for yourself.* It was time to call the one person on earth who made her feel accepted. She walked back into her apartment, sat on the falling-apart sofa, and lit up the first cigarette of the day. She then called her grandmother.

"Hi *Bubbe*."

"Tammy, what a sweet surprise."

"I'm so sorry about, you know, about …"

"Sugar, you don't have to be bashful about it. I have breast cancer—you can say it."

She wasn't going to say it. That would make it real. "How are you feeling? Are you in pain? What—what's going to happen now?"

"They want me to have what they call a lumpectomy. It sounds awful, doesn't it?"

"When?"

"This Monday. Monday morning."

"Monday? That's so soon." Tamara tried to remember her schedule. "I wish I could be there."

"Could you? It would mean the world to me. I just got off the phone with your mother—"

"She's worried about me, right?"

"What's troubling you, sugar? Like with your mother, I could always tell when something was troubling her, And now she's troubled about you. She doesn't understand, now that you've graduated, why you don't just come home. Tell me what it is, Tammy."

"I don't belong in this world. There's no place for me here."

"It's a boy, isn't it?"

Tamara answered with uncontrolled sobbing.

Helen quickly responded, "Rejection causes so much pain, doesn't it, sweetheart?"

"How'd you know?"

"No one told me a thing, but I know when your mother cried like this, it was always because some boy she liked didn't like her. It's hard being a woman. I'm old now, but I remember always being so worried—was I pretty? And afraid I wasn't. That blind date with your grandfather. Oooh, I was so scared. My ugly hair and I knew I was too fat. I'm glad in a way that Saul isn't here anymore, may he rest in peace. If he were here, I'd be so worried about what I'd look like after this surgery."

"Aw, *Bubbe*, I love you."

"Tammy, please come and visit me. You would do a world of good for me—for your mother also. You know, right now your mother is feeling rejected, too."

"But that's crazy—it's not Mom I'm rejecting—it's—sorry, I shouldn't go into this. But if you want me to come and visit—I mean are you going to need someone to be with you, maybe to help out or something?"

"Would you do that for me? With your mother having to drive all the way from Boca to Miami—I can't ask her to do that." A pause, then Helen asked, "Would you stay with me?"

"Yes, I would." The idea of her grandmother being all alone until her surgery was just too sad—and Tamara would make sure it didn't happen that way. "How about I leave now? I could be at your condo by maybe dinnertime."

"I'll get the bed ready for you."

Once the call ended, Tamara stared at her phone. What did she need to take care of before making this quick getaway? She needed her to-do list. She grabbed it from the top of the refrigerator and sat. Poised to write, she realized there was very little to do.

Might as well face it—I don't have much of a life here anyway. No one is going to notice I'm gone. Maybe my landlord and my boss at that dinky job.

Her phone lit up with Jesse's snarky smile filling the screen. "Hello."

"I got one question. Do you believe that crazy stuff your parents believe? Dad explained it all to me and—wow!"

Not fair. It was her parents' faith—not hers. "No, I don't. I don't know what I believe, okay? Can you handle that?"

"So, what were you doing showing up at my *shul*? I mean, hey, Tamara, I loved seeing you there. Man, when I recognized you from class—truth is I had an eye on you already. And wow there you were."

"I was surprised—and glad—when I saw you there, too ... but not so glad last night—I kept looking at you to defend me, but, Jesse, you just sat there!"

"What did you want me to do? I didn't know what was going on. I thought maybe your Dad was an ax murderer or something. I still don't understand why you visited my *shul* if you and your family are Christians? Maybe you were stalking me—and tried passing yourself off as a regular Jew."

"Ha, that's where you're wrong. There's nothing regular about me."

His laugh was even more snarky than his smile, but laughter was a welcoming sound and the tension around her neck and shoulders began to ease. She rolled her head in a complete circle to work out the knots. With a sigh, she sat on her secondhand sofa.

"Listen, Jesse, I came to Temple Beth El cause I wasn't sure but thought maybe I'd feel like that's where I belonged."

"I always wondered why you didn't come back."

"The synagogue made me feel empty. I don't belong anywhere."

"Not true. Face it, you belong with me."

Should she fall for this? Heat rose to her cheeks, yet quickly a steel wall clamped down on her heart. As *Bubbe* had said, rejection hurts, so why bother? "Listen, I gotta go. I'm leaving to go see my *Bubbe* in Miami."

"Why? Because of me?"

"No, silly goose. *Bubbe's* got cancer so I'm leaving to take care of her. And she's a regular Jew—okay?

"No! You can't leave now. I just stood up to my Dad and told him I was going to continue seeing you. He's mad, but I think he'll come around—at least I hope he does so he'll finance our movie when we get rolling on it. Hey, you know what? Miami has a great film school. Huh? What do you think about us checking it out? Huh?"

"Right now I'm worried about my Grandmother. She's the only grandmother I have—actually the only grandparent I have—at least the only one I have a relationship with. My Mom's Dad died and my Dad's parents won't talk to us—for the same reason your father doesn't like me."

"Okay, yeah, I get it. It's gotta be hard for you, what with your parents' nutty religion, but still, Tammy, think about looking into the film school. Would you?"

"I guess. Maybe. And maybe you could come and visit the campus with me?"

Chapter Nine

House of David

aomi eyed the obligatory dour-looking dress. She lifted it out of the closet and held it in front of her. Glimpsing herself from the mirror, she groaned and rolled her eyes. "Ugh." Blousy, drab, and plain. What could she do? The oldest woman in the congregation presented it to her as a birthday gift and probably expected her to be wearing it tonight.

She checked the clock on Daniel's nightstand—there was enough time to steal a few moments at her secret place before dressing for tonight's Shabbat service.

She hung the dress back up, then tiptoed past Daniel's study to the hallway closet. Naomi reached behind the beach towels and retrieved Daniel's guitar. He hadn't touched it in several years, un-aware it had become Naomi's treasure. Thankfully Naomi inherited her mother's ear for music and despite not having had lessons, tunes emerged as she plucked the strings.

Naomi's rose garden's gurgling fountain calmed her mind and prepared her to encounter the living God. She strummed and her heart poured out the words.

Yeshua, My Beloved
I was made to love You
I was made to adore You
You hold me as no other
Know me as no other
My Beloved
More lovely than ten thousand

You have given me beyond measure. This home, this security, this husband, but I'm empty. Have I sinned against You?

If she could, she would wait for His voice, but not tonight. She must go and put on that dress and a smile. She returned the guitar to its hiding place and soon was wearing both the dress and the smile. One last look in the mirror. *Oh, Mrs. Cantor, that smile is just way too plastic. Liven it up, girl.*

But where was Daniel? He should be in here dressing. Down the hallway to his study. It was getting too late to knock—she broke her self-imposed rule of always knocking, Tonight she simply walked in.

"You're not dressed yet. What's the matter?"

With a swoop of his arm, he waved a sea of crumpled paper off his desk and onto the floor. "Torah portion tonight is on the red heifer—Numbers 19. There is definitely something I can do from that—I'm thinking maybe how the red heifer had to be outside the camp—but then there's the Haftorah portion from Micah. How do I do justice to both of these portions along with reading from the New Covenant?"

"Daniel, I've asked you before, why are you still doing Torah portions? We're not at a *shul* anymore. Besides which you seem more stressed than usual?"

"Sam's coming tonight. Remember?" He stood and grabbed his Bible and a few sheets of paper. "We'd better get going." Looking at her for the first time, he noted, "You're wearing the dress Goldie gave you—it suits you."

After another eye roll, Naomi did the finishing touches to her makeup as she waited for Daniel. He came to the bathroom door and said, "Come on, you're going to make us late."

"Me?" She caught herself before calling out his behavior. Why did Daniel always have to get so nervous around Sam? She blotted her lips and turned her head both ways to ensure that her makeup made up for the dress, then headed to the front door where Daniel was now waiting. She passed by him just as the phone rang.

Seeing her turn back to answer it, he grabbed her arm, "Let's go, we don't have time."

"Let me just see who it is," She headed back to check the caller ID. *Mom.* Without regard for how Daniel might react, she picked up the phone. "Mom, are you okay? We're on our way to House of David right now."

"Yes, dear, I'm fine."

"Oh good. Let me call you when we get back."

Daniel walked to the phone and said into it, "Yes, Mom, we're leaving,"

Naomi, the phone still in Daniel's hand, could hear her mother say, "I just wanted to let you know that Tamara is coming tomorrow for a stay with me."

Naomi's heart dropped, unable to process the idea.

"We'll call you later, Mom. We gotta go now."

Daniel drove faster than Naomi cared for, but that didn't interrupt her soliloquy. "Why didn't she call me? I can't believe she's coming back and not even calling me. She hates me." At a traffic light, she touched his shoulder and said "Can you give me some help, please. I need your help, Daniel."

"Naomi, I need yours, too? What do you think I should focus on tonight? I know it's late, but I can always improvise. You never give me your input anymore."

"Okay, but you're probably not going to like it."

"Go on."

"Okay, here goes. Skip the red heifer and go right to the Micah passage. I remember a couple of years ago talking to Mrs. Adelson. When she told me, 'if you can show me how Jesus is God, maybe then I'll believe,' I read to her from Micah 2. And now she's a Believer. I mean why do you feel you still have to do all this rabbi stuff?"

He pulled into First Baptist's parking lot and asked, "Did you bring your tambourine?"

"Of course, I always bring it. Stop putting yourself under all this pressure."

Another car door slammed and Sam Needleman called out to them.

He must have been lurking here waiting to pounce on my husband.

Daniel put his arm around Naomi's waist. "Smile. He's been very good to us. Don't forget—."

"I know ... We still have our house." Naomi quickly forced her frown into a broad smile. "*Shabbat Shalom*, Sam."

"Always a pleasure to see you, Naomi." Sam approached Daniel, patted his upper arm while shaking his hand. After scanning the number of cars in the parking lot, he nodded. "Looks like a good crowd. Good choice you made renting this place. Great location. Oh, and I like the beard on you. Very nice."

Inside everyone smiled and greeted them with *Shabbat Shalom*. Naomi smiled and nodded her head but held off on returning the customary greeting. She took her customary—first row with Daniel.

To signal the start of service, Henry came forward with his prayer shawl draped around his shoulders and blew the shofar. He was a quiet gentle man from Jamaica who asked that he be called Mordechai. He adopted the Hebrew name because, as he explained it, he wanted to be identified as a Jew. More than half the congregation were Gentile yet striving to be more Jewish than Daniel or Naomi.

Daniel rose, walked to the podium, and led the congregation in reciting the *Shema*[4], first in Hebrew and then in English. After Daniel led the recitation of the Messianic Apostles' Creed, came the candle lighting, then the blessing over the wine and bread, and

---

4 Shema (Hebrew: "Hear"). This is considered to be the Jewish confession of faith, taken from Deut. 6:4-9, 11:13-21, and Numbers 15:37-41."Hear O Israel: the LORD is our God, the LORD is One. You shall love the Lord your God with all your heart, with all your soul, and with all your strength."

then forty-five minutes of worship with singing and dancing, And finally time to squeeze in the message.

Daniel chose to continue the discussion-style format he had instituted at Temple Beth Shalom. Soon people were asking question after question about the red heifer.

If Naomi heard one more person say "Rabbi, I hear they're breeding one now," she would scream. *What does that have to do with Yeshua?*

Finally, it was time for the offering and following that, the Aaronic Benediction. After Daniel finished inviting everyone to partake of the delicious foods brought by members of the congregation, he left the podium and walked toward Naomi. With an imperceptible shrug of his shoulders, he raised his eyebrows and forced a slight grin. "Never did get to Micah, did I?"

Before Naomi could say, "And not the New Testament either," Sam inserted himself between the couple and whispered, "Daniel, you need to cover the cross that's up there. I'm surprised you haven't done that already. We have spoken about this."

Cover up the cross!?!

"Excuse me," Naomi said as she picked up her purse and her tambourine. "I'm going to enjoy some of the chicken someone brought."

After their last smile and thank you, the exhausted couple headed for the refuge of their automobile. They buckled up as Sam walked past the car. Naomi smiled and waved as she said between her teeth, "Cover the cross? You're not going to listen to him, are you?"

"Let's wait 'til we get home to talk about this, okay?"

Naomi knew better than to try to force the conversation. Daniel backed the car up, steered past Sam's car, and finally drove out from the parking lot. One hand loosening his tie and the other gripping the steering wheel, Daniel said, "Sam suggests we could put the Israeli flag or a banner with the Star of David over the cross. I'll let you decide—flag or star?"

"Yeshua wasn't nailed to a flag or to the Jewish star, or am I wrong, Rabbi?"

Daniel turned his head fully toward Naomi. "You want to be truly Biblical about it—He was nailed to a tree, Naomi." A car horn caused Daniel to yank the steering wheel to avoid hitting a car in the lane he had veered into.

"Daniel!"

"Now you see why I wanted to wait until we got home."

"Go ahead, blame me."

Naomi turned her head to hide her tears. Once home, Daniel broke tradition, leaving her sitting in the car rather than walking over to her side and opening the door for her. After the sting of rejection, she let herself out and walked to her secret place in the rose garden. She gazed at the crescent moon, contemplating the vastness of her Lord. Sometimes this helped expand the smallness of her world and its problems, but rather to appreciate the intimacy she could share with the Creator of everything.

By the time she came into the house, Daniel was already asleep. Knowing she was not ready to surrender to sleep, she went into Daniel's study. Rich with an amber leather couch, a mahogany desk, and books encompassing the walls, it was a sanctuary. A place where she could both curl up and kneel down.

With all the devotionals neatly stacked up on the bookshelf, she was trying to decide what book to choose from, when Daniel opened the door and came to her. Taking her hand, he said, "I promised you we could talk when we got home and instead I left you sitting in the car."

"You've never done anything like that to me before."

The palm of his hand wiped away her tears. "It was what the talk would be about. I'm not ready ... My-omi, I sometimes feel that we are doing—the Friday night services, the Torah portions, the—"

"the *Shema.*"

"No. not the *Shema*. But the other things. Even the candle lighting ..." His voice broke as he continued, "Sometimes they feel empty. Like a ritual I'm expected to do."

She wrapped her arms around his neck and hugged him. "Yes, I—"

"No, you don't ..." Daniel led her to the couch. When both were seated, he kissed her forehead. "Honey, I can't do the Gentile thing. I'm a Jew. We have ancestors who died with the *Shema* on their lips, refusing to be converted by the ones calling themselves Christians? I know Yeshua is our Messiah, and I know our people—most of them—have rejected Him, but I can't reject my people."

Chapter Ten

Water from a Rock

D riving south on I-75, the pink glow to Tamara's left, although it was a beautiful sunset it signaled she would be disappointing *Bubbe*. The woman probably fussed and fussed over making dinner for her, but by now she was wondering if her granddaughter was ever going to really come.

I want to be there for you, Bubbe, I really do. Yeshua, help me get there soon—and safely.

Yeshua. The Name she was taught to worship, yet at college, no one used His Hebrew Name. She tried church once, but it was of no use—it was like wearing someone else's shoes, a stranger in a strange land—added to it was the vision of her father seeing her in a church! And this was where the idea of attending a synagogue was born. *Jesse. Could I ever just be Jewish and be accepted? Plain old Jewish.*

If she thought about her *Bubbe*, Jewishness was the very essence of the dear woman. And oh how *Bubbe* loved Israel. If a friend of *Bubbe's* died, without question, the friend would be memorialized with a new tree planted in Israel. *Bubbe* with her Hersh Siegel and Moishe Kermish. And, after all, Tamara called her "*Bubbe*," not granny. And for dinner tonight most definitely there would be matzoh ball soup and hopefully her made-from-scratch rugelach.

But what about *Bubbe's* husband? The one she never met. The one that made *Bubbe* have to sneak away if she wanted to visit with her daughter and her grandchildren. You can't leave out that part of being Jewish either. Whether her family said Yeshua or Jesus, it didn't matter. Rejection is rejection.

But here I am rejecting the One that connects me to God. If I didn't know that I had a Savior, One who loved me, I'd be left completely alone. I'd have no relationship to my God. I can't do that. I can't reject Yeshua. I need Him.

The sun was almost completely set by the time she pulled into the parking garage under *Bubbe*'s condo. Out of the elevator and not even at the front door yet, Tamara could smell the brisket and the distinct fragrance of freshly baked bread.

"I'm so sorry I'm late, it—.

"Oh, sugar, you're here, that's all that matters. You must be starving."

"I am, but I hope you didn't wait for me to eat."

"Of course, I did. Sit sweetheart. I've kept the soup warm."

It was delicious. The freshly baked challah, the brisket … everything. Yet best of all was the warming love and acceptance that melted Tamara's sharp edges.

Dinner over, Tamara insisted *Bubbe* sit down and relax, while Tamara cleaned up. Once finished, she joined *Bubbe* in the living room. "I'll never have your kitchen as clean as you keep it."

"Never worry about that, sweetheart. But I need to talk to you about something."

"Sure. What?"

"Once Saul was gone, I started having a little schnapps after dinner and before going to sleep. Would you like some with me?

"What's schnapps?"

"It's alcohol, Tammy, it started with Saul when he gave me some schnapps to drink. The only time I had alcohol before that was at Passover." She paused, put her hand over her mouth and shook her head. "I told a lie—when I sang at those dance marathons I did drink some, but never schnapps. Saul told me that if I had the peach one, it'd be much easier to drink. It's sweet." Helen giggled, "even when it burns."

94

"How can I resist—such a new adventure, thanks, *Bubbe.* Tell me where it is, and I'll pour for both of us."

While pouring a second glass for both, Tamara asked, "You never told me about a dance marathon—what was that?"

"They were contests during the depression. Couples would dance til they couldn't do more than just walk. They'd go for hours. All for a few dollars. And I'd try to sing as loud and as full of life as I could to help them stay awake. Did I ever tell you how I learned to sing?" When Tamara shook her head, *Bubbe* continued. "I've told these stories to your mother so much, I guess it's time I bored you with them. You see, growing up in Alabama—."

"How did you end up in Alabama? I thought all Jews never left New York – unless it was to go to Florida when they got old. Ouch, I'm sorry."

"My parents were farmers in the old country, sweetheart. They went to Texas first and then ended up in Montgomery. And down south they didn't like us Jews very much. We had to live in the bad side of town. Our next-door neighbors ran a brothel. And from their window, I heard the radio." Helen leapt into song, her feet tapping and her head bouncing with the beat. "St. Louis Woman, wid her diamond rings ..." She abruptly stopped and blushed. "I'm sorry, I shouldn't have—."

"Are you kidding? I loved it. You have to promise to sing more for me while I'm staying with you. So, *Bubbe,* is that where you met my grandfather—at one of those marathons?"

"Oh, sweetheart, Saul came a little later. I was an old maid by that time. All my sisters were married and I had to stay and take care of my mother. I was 36 when I met Saul. He was a New Yorker. A Jew working on the Air Force Base in Montgomery. Jews were never permitted at the Base until Saul—he was a tailor for them. My brother introduced us. The first New Yorker I ever met. And before going back to New York, he told me he'd write me. I never thought he would, but he did, and with the second letter he sent me a paper cigar ring with a plane ticket to New York." She reached across her end table, picked up a framed photograph, and handed it to Tamara. "See, he always had a pipe in his mouth. I wish you could have met him. I begged him, but he … well, he was a New Yorker. Only when Saul was away somewhere, could I meet you, your brother, and your mother." With tears suddenly spilling down her cheeks, she reached for a tissue from the same end table. "I had to meet my daughter and my grandchildren in secret."

"Because of my parents' faith, right? See, that's why I don't get it. Why do we have to be so different?"

Bubbe bit her lip, took a sip remaining in her glass of schnapps. "Tell me about this boy."

Tamara welcomed the opportunity to talk about Jesse … their dreams of making a film, Mr. Steinberg, all the way to Jesse's curly hair and snarky smile. *Bubbe,* without one comment, listened. Until a yawn escaped.

"Oh, *Bubbe*, I'm sorry. I've been going on and we need to get you ready for tomorrow."

"I wish I could wait til Monday, sleep in my own bed another night before they cut me up, but they said I had to come Sunday."

"We need to be there by ten, right?" She helped her grandmother rise from her cushy couch and walked her to her bedroom. "That schnapps should really help you sleep tonight, huh? Before I get too drunk on this stuff, I'll clean up and have everything ready for tomorrow."

Before saying good night, Helen cupped Tamara's face and told her, "Stop seeing that boy. He's not good for you."

"But, *Bubbe* …"

"And sweetheart, you need to call your mother. I want both my girls to be with me at the hospital. Please."

Walking Naomi to the front door, Daniel heard how hard it was raining. "Wait a minute, let me get you the umbrella." Once he had opened it, he escorted Naomi to her car.

"Stop worrying about me—I know you get nervous when I drive into Miami, but I'll be fine."

"You sure? Even with the rain?"

Rolling her eyes, she nodded. "Yes, I'm sure. Once I get to the hospital, I'll call you to let you know I'm fine. Okay?"

"I'd appreciate it." He tipped the umbrella away from the car door and kissed her. "Tell Tamara I'm proud of her for asking you to be there today. I told you she'd call you."

"Nah. It wasn't really her idea. I'm sure it was Mom's. Bye, honey. I'll call you."

Sunday was usually a day the couple chose to be their Sabbath. Friday from sundown until Saturday at sundown really couldn't work as their day of rest as it actually was a workday. And usually Daniel would not begin preparing his Sabbath message until perhaps Tuesday. This Sunday, however, with Naomi not being home, he was looking forward to closing himself off in his study and digging into the Scriptures.

The Torah portion for the next service would be from Numbers 20.

> *Then came the children of Israel, even the whole congregation, into the desert of Zin in the first month: and the people abode in Kadesh; and Miriam died there, and was buried there.*
> *And there was no water for the congregation: and they gathered themselves together against Moses and against Aaron.*
> *And the people chode with Moses, and spake, saying, Would God that we had died when our brethren died before the* Lord!
> *And why have ye brought up the congregation of the* Lord *into this wilderness, that we and our cattle should die there?*
> *And wherefore have ye made us to come up out of Egypt, to bring us in unto this evil place? it is no place of seed, or of figs,*

or of vines, or of pomegranates; neither is there any water to drink.

And Moses and Aaron went from the presence of the assembly unto the door of the tabernacle of the congregation, and they fell upon their faces: and the glory of the Lord appeared unto them.

And the Lord spake unto Moses, saying,

Take the rod, and gather thou the assembly together, thou, and Aaron thy brother, and speak ye unto the rock before their eyes; and it shall give forth his water, and thou shalt bring forth to them water out of the rock: so thou shalt give the congregation and their beasts drink.

And Moses took the rod from before the Lord, as he commanded him.

And Moses and Aaron gathered the congregation together before the rock, and he said unto them, Hear now, ye rebels; must we fetch you water out of this rock?

And Moses lifted up his hand, and with his rod he smote the rock twice: and the water came out abundantly, and the congregation drank, and their beasts also.

And the Lord spake unto Moses and Aaron, Because ye believed me not, to sanctify me in the eyes of the children of Israel, therefore ye shall not bring this congregation into the land which I have given them

Daniel pushed his chair away from the desk and fell to his knees. "Oh Lord God, forgive me. I read this and know I have angered you more than Moses did. I speak your Word to others—I teach. But You know, Lord, I can't love You with all my heart as You command and as I teach others. My heart is like stone but I don't know why. I believe Yeshua is the Messiah. But it's all in my head, not in my heart. I wish I could love You the way my wife does. Please, Lord, change me. Make me into who I pretend to be."

On her way home from the hospital that day, Naomi surprised Daniel with Chinese takeout. As they were together setting the table, he asked, "So, how was time with Tamara?"

"Strained," With her index finger to her lips, her eyes avoiding his, she asked, "Can I tell you about something kinda amazing that happened today?"

Her tone of voice told him he probably didn't want to hear this, but a man learns. He smiled and arched his eyebrows. *Go ahead.*

"You know how we've talked that Mom needed to accept the Lord before surgery?"

He nodded, eyebrows arched.

"When I said to Mom that she needed Yeshua, you know what she said to me?"

Everything set to eat, he pulled out a chair for Naomi. "No, but must not have been good. You don't look happy."

"Mom said, 'Oh, that's what Saul did before he died.' It seems a nurse before Dad had his final heart attack, led him to ask Jesus into his heart—Mom said clearly the nurse had used the name Jesus—not Yeshua."

"You're frowning. Are you afraid he wasn't sincere enough?"

"I hope he was, but, Daniel, all the prophecy we showed him, and made sure he knew we observed the Jewish holidays—none of that got through to him. But when he heard the Gospel ..." Naomi snapped her fingers.

He put his fork down and lifted his napkin from his lap and onto the table. "We keep the traditions, we say Yeshua and not Jesus—because we need to reach our own people."

"But all the people who come to our congregation are Gentiles—most of them anyway."

"Thanks for bringing the Chinese." He left the table and picked up the car keys.

"Don't you want to hear about how things went with Tamara and all? And how Mom is doing?"

Obviously, he didn't. The front door opened and quickly slammed shut.

After making a half-hearted attempt to put the food into plastic containers, Naomi chose to match her actions with her emotions. The lo mein and the moo shu pork were gobbled up by the garbage disposal.

A paralyzing aloneness engulfed her. It was years ago, but hopefully her friend hadn't changed her phone number, and thankfully Melinda answered on the first ring.

"Naomi?. How are you? How is your husband's congregation going?"

"Uh—that's a long … Melinda, you were such a good counselor. I was just wondering … I need counseling again, but not, you know, because of the abortion, but … well, maybe actually do you do any couple counseling?"

"No, but I know a few who do. But they're Christians."

"That's good."

"But they're only Christian, not Jewish ones."

Naomi gasped. "Is this why we lost touch? Cause we're different … cause you're not Jewish?

"Well, yeah, in a way. I was always nervous that I'd say something wrong. I tried being careful to always say Yeshua, but one time James said Jesus or something that seemed to upset Daniel."

More silence, until Melinda, always sensitive and intuitive, offered, "Would you like to meet sometime? Maybe tomorrow? I'd love to see you again."

"I wish I could tomorrow, but my Mom is having surgery tomorrow morning."

Chapter Eleven

Why Bother?

Naomi, Tamara, and Zac held hands around Helen's hospital bed. Wearing his prayer shawl, Daniel's hands graced Helen's head.

"May the Holy One of Israel hear our prayers for our beloved Ora." Daniel leaned into Helen's ear. "Do you mind my using your Hebrew name, Mom?"

Helen's smile expressed her consent and her delight.

Daniel continued. "Grant her faith to know that You are with her. Give guidance to her medical team and restore her to health so that she may speedily return to us, as we love her dearly. Let us all say Amen."

Daniel kissed his mother-in-law's forehead. Helen held a few of the tassels from his blue *Tallit*[5] and kissed them. She then looked to the rest of the family, beaming a shy smile. "My own personal rabbi. I am a blessed woman."

As he removed the *Tallit* from his shoulders and began folding it, Naomi put out her hand. "Let me."

Daniel handed it to her with a surprised smile. She whispered, "I love you." As she then ceremonially folded the shawl, Tamara reached into her mother's purse and found the blue velvet pouch her father always used to place this folded garment and handed it to her mother. As a little girl, Tamara loved watching her parents perform this ritual. Daniel wrapped his wife and daughter in his arms and told Helen, "And, Mom, I am a blessed man."

---

5 Fringed Prayer Shawl

The heavy wooden door swung open. "Hello, Mrs. Goldblatt,"

"Is it time?" Naomi asked as a nurse entered the room.

"The anesthesiologist and his team are on their way. I'll show you where the surgical waiting room is."

Once in the waiting room, Daniel spied the coffee. "Hope it's strong."

Naomi offered, "I'll fix a cup for both of us. What you did for Mom, was special to her."

With his characteristic arched eyebrows, he asked, "Not too Jewish for you?"

She gave his arm a playful slap, as the thunderous ringtone of Red Hot Chili Peppers blasted from Tamara's phone. Daniel shook his head, glaring at his daughter. Thankfully, Tamara quickly answered.

"Hey, Jesse." Tamara rose and began leaving the room. However, after two steps into the hallway, she was back, grabbed her purse and left once again.

Zac smirked. "Cigarettes. I'll bet you anything." Zac picked up his phone and said, "I'll go out there with her and give the radio station a call. And afterward, I'll try talking with Tam. Mind my playing Dad for a minute?"

"You've always done a good job taking care of your sister. I'm proud of you," said the real Dad.

Without a table for her coffee, Naomi placed it on the floor by her feet. She subtly glanced down the hallway and once assured that neither of the twins was returning to the room, she placed her hand on Daniel's knee. "Can I ask you something?"

"Why do I think I'm being set up?" He smiled, and said, "Ask."

"What I said the other day about Dad, you know, how he said a prayer with the nurse, is that why you didn't tell Mom about Yeshua today?"

"Haven't you noticed, I don't do that anymore? Whether it's your mother, or anyone else if they're Jewish."

"But why?"

"It's an affront, Naomi. They associate the name of our Messiah with someone who caused their persecution." Daniel walked to the coffee machine and poured another cup. "Besides, why bother?"

Her jaw dropping, she asked, "Why bother?"

"They all reject what we tell them. They rejected Him two thousand years ago, and they still do."

Jumping up quickly, Naomi bumped into her hot cup of coffee. "No!"

She ran to get a paper towel, but Daniel, seeing her hands were shaking, followed her and said, "Honey, I'll take care of it. Go sit back down." While on the floor mopping up the spill, he looked up and asked, "For now, can you simply be satisfied that I'm conducting *Shabbat* services? I'd like to believe that's all the Lord requires of me. It'll have to do."

He rose, walked to a wastebasket, and threw in the paper towels. He came back and sat alongside Naomi, cupping her face. "Naomi, my parents don't even talk to us. Our children have never gotten to know them. Then there's your father. Maybe before he died he said something, maybe he's in heaven, but never not once did he talk to his grandchildren. That's how most of our people feel about Yeshua. They yelled 'crucify Him' then and today they yell crucify *us*. Yeshua told them their house would be desolate."

"Why continue with House of David then?"

"What else can I do to support us?" As her back stiffened, Daniel softened his voice. "We'll work this out."

"Daniel, can I ask you something?"

"You're going to ask anyway, so go ahead."

"Melinda mentioned that maybe—I mean I asked her, she didn't just mention it out of the blue—I asked if she knew a good marriage counselor—not that we need one or anything, but would you consider, maybe?"

Zac and Tamara burst into the room, both asking, "Has the doctor been here yet?"

Perfect timing, Dr. Abadi, still wearing his scrubs, smiled, and said, "Here I am. Mrs. Goldblatt is now in recovery. They will tell you when you can see her."

Tamara asked, "How did she do?"

The dark-haired young man turned to Tamara and smiled. "She did fine. And once the biopsy is done, we will meet for a consultation, with whoever Mrs. Goldblatt would like to be a part of this meeting."

His warm smile and direct gaze toward Tamara must have been why her cheeks pinkened. As Dr. Abadi left the room, Zac nudged his sister. "Is it getting hot in here for you, Tammy?"

"Shut up, Zac."

While the siblings had their fun, Daniel quietly told Naomi, "Yes."

Tamara immediately asked, "Yes? Yes to what?"

Zac jumped right in, "Yes, to my sister's making googoo eyes with the doc."

"Shut up, Zac."

Daniel took Naomi's hand and said, "Yes, to the counselor."

Chapter Twelve

For I Know the Plans I Have for You

"*Bubbe*, I'm going out to your lanai for a few."

Helen delicately lifted herself from the sofa and started for her bedroom. "Yes, sweetheart, enjoy your cigarette."

Tamara frowned as she observed how carefully Helen moved, almost as if frightened to lift her left arm. Earlier today Tamara had made the mistake of asking *Bubbe* to turn on the lamp on the end table. Helen, in doing so, winced.

Once on the terrace, Tamara quickly reached for the pack of cigarettes she had placed on the PVC table earlier in the day. *Bubbe* had told her to not worry if she needed to smoke, yet it was easy to see that the smell caused *Bubbe's* face to unwillingly form a scowl. It could have been the opportunity to stop her "nasty habit" as her mother called it, but Tamara shrugged this thought away—she had just too much to deal with right now. If anything, at least she had cut back to almost half what she normally smoked in a day. Lighting up, she leaned over the railing and found the warm ocean breeze invited a few moments of necessary reflection.

This time here in Miami, being a dutiful granddaughter, was really only a brief interlude. A fulfilling one, yet one that could be all-encompassing and cause her to forget her empty meaningless directionless life.

Film school? She did love the medium of film to tell a story, with so many creative ways to tell the story, but what was the story? What was the message? Did she have one? Did you need to have a message to make a film? Of course not. Just a story. A good one. Where she would be playing the lead.

But would that make her happy? She knew it wouldn't. How could she deny the paralyzing sense of emptiness after a curtain call when she had the lead in a high school play.

Maybe not having anyone to share that moment with was the cause for the emptiness. Maybe all she's really ever wanted was a boyfriend. From an early age, she would watch her parents, how they were so connected. Mom always anticipating Dad's needs and Dad always with this enamored expression on his face when he was looking at Mom.

Not any relationship obviously would fill the emptiness—only one that she grew up watching.

Was it her parents' faith? Did that make the difference?

No, forget it, I'm not going there.

She stubbed out her cigarette. Guess she should go back in and check on *Bubbe*. Why doesn't she take a pain pill when she needs one? That's why they make the pills after all. You feel pain, you pop a pill. And what about *Bubbe* saying "I'm not having that horrible chemotherapy. My friend Esther was sick as a dog when she had that."

And no matter how Tamara pleaded with her, she wouldn't budge--no chemo and no radiation either. Wasn't it her responsibility to basically manage *Bubbe's* health? Maybe she could call Dr. Abadi.

The thought was just too thrilling—thrilling enough to make her question her motives. The morning he came into Helen's hospital room the day before surgery, Tamara was surprised. Dr. Abadi was so young. So warm. So soft-spoken. So handsome. She had to admit dark-haired exotic-looking men were the ones she was always drawn to. Jesse? Blonde curly hair and snarky.

She even found it charming the way the doctor removed the tortoiseshell glasses when talking directly to his patient. He had a trace of a mysterious accent, too. Intriguing. Where does he come from?

Yikes, what if he's Muslim? My parents would disown me. But that's not the point. It's not about me. But … but … no matter the motive, it could help *Bubbe* if I talk to him. She walked back inside, snatched up her phone, and tiptoed into the kitchen. Removing the doctor's card from the refrigerator door, she immediately called his office.

She was told it would be about two hours before the doctor could call her back, leaving her the need to figure out how to not be anywhere near *Bubbe* when he called. In two hours, it would be near dinnertime. While considering her options, she walked to *Bubbe's* bedroom and was surprised to see she was coming back out to the living room.

"*Bubbe*, I was just about to go into your room. You want me to get you anything?"

"No, sweetheart. It's time for *Name that Tune*, it's my favorite show. I never miss it, but I almost slept through it tonight. Come, watch with me."

"Sure."

Helen picked up the TV remote, sat at the end of the sofa, and patted the cushion next to her. "Try and guess with me."

"Oh, you'll probably guess them all before I even open my mouth." She sat next to her and with a hug, said, "You're really good at this, aren't you?"

"Sometimes, I've guessed it by the second note. Saul was always amazed. Wanted me to get on the show. Said I'd make us a fortune. I told him probably with all the lights and cameras, I'd get too flustered."

"Yeah, I can imagine. *Bubbe*, what would you want for dinner? I was thinking maybe I could go out and get some Chinese for both of us. Would you like that?"

"I don't think I'll be too hungry. I don't feel like eating much. But you can get for yourself. I'll give you some money."

"But you need to eat more. Ever since the surgery, you haven't eaten hardly at all." Tamara kissed her on the cheek. "Please, for me."

"Maybe some wonton soup. And maybe an egg roll." Seeing the show was about to begin, she turned up the volume on the remote. "It's just starting."

And just like *Bubbe* had said, two maybe three notes and she named that tune. Every time.

Timing seemed to work out perfectly. The quiz show lasted thirty minutes and with Tamara taking her time dressing to go out, by the time she was in the car driving to a restaurant, her phone rang.

Tamara was warmed by Dr. Abadi immediately remembering her. "Is everything all right with Mrs. Goldblatt—with your grandmother?"

"Well, not really."

"Oh?"

"Yes, Doctor Abadi, first of all, she told me she won't go along with having chemotherapy, nor even the radiation treatment."

"I understand your concern, but give her time. She's scared…"

"But I'm scared, too. I don't want her to—"

"Please, may I explain? I must tell you, when I first began practicing medicine, I found myself getting very upset—people just didn't always make the right choices. They said 'no' when they should have said 'yes', some didn't take their medicine. The worst was a patient who had lung cancer, but he still smoked, wouldn't give it up, no matter how much I tried to convince him. When I stepped back and realized our God gives us free will, then I had to ask myself who did I think I was to force someone to do what they don't want to do."

"But this is my grandmother. And the second thing is she is in pain. I can tell, but she refuses to take any pain pills. I can't not do something."

"You can pray for your grandmother—your *Bubbe*, as I heard you call her. That's actually what I learned to do. Especially the man with lung cancer. I prayed for him and eventually all on his own he came to me and asked for something to help him quit smoking. And he quit. No matter how much you love someone, you can't take away their free will."

Reminding Tamara of one of her father's messages, she said, "Makes me think of Pharaoh and how he hardened his heart. Does that make sense to you?"

With a quiet chuckle, he told her it did. "And I will pray for your grandmother."

Tamara was stunned by this man's words, said with a trace of an accent—one she couldn't identify. "Would you mind if I asked what country you were from?"

With another chuckle, he told her, "Egypt."

"Oh … well, we will see you for *Bubbe's* follow-up visit. And, yes, if you can pray about her, that would be great—I mean very kind."

Immediately after hanging up, she slapped her forehead with her hand. "Tamara, you had to mention Pharaoh. Good grief—the guy's Egyptian." She was interrupted from beating herself up by her phone ringing. Jesse's face filled the screen. With only a slight hesitation, Tamara hit decline.

Chapter Thirteen

Making It Personal

ith two hours before they needed to leave for their first counseling session, at Daniel's suggestion, he and Naomi were enjoying their swimming pool. Daniel doing laps. Naomi doing the water aerobics learned from their gym.

On his last lap, Daniel dove under, butterflied to Naomi, and grabbed her ankles. After a playful splashing contest, they climbed the ladder out of the pool. While Daniel dried himself with a towel, Naomi ran toward him and shook the water off herself and onto Daniel.

"Oh no, you don't." He took his towel and wrapped it around her and made the point of drying her hair before she could dowse him with any more water. Pointing with his chin to their double chaise lounge, he said, "Come on. Let's talk."

Once seated, he asked, "Naomi, what exactly are we going to be talking about with this *stranger?*"

She was expecting this. With a placid voice, she reminded him, "You already agreed, Daniel."

"I know, but—"

"But what?"

"I love you. I've never stopped. What the tension between us is … look, I feel I know what it is, and I just don't see why we can't talk this out. Naomi, why can't we work this out by ourselves?"

She wouldn't admit it to him, but she also was contemplating how awkward it would be to expose their relationship to a stranger. For twenty-five years they had journeyed together. Their rhythms, their nuances, their private jokes, as well as their sore spots—no one should try to rip open their one flesh. She acquiesced, "We can try if you want."

"It all has to do with House of David, doesn't it? You resent it."

The edge to his voice reminded Naomi of the rejection she experienced when he had left her in the car after last week's *Shabat* service.

Intuitively he said, "I'm sorry, I never apologized to you for the other night when I left you sitting in the car." He placed his fingers on her quivering lips as tears traveled down her cheeks. "I really hurt you—will you forgive me?"

The tears turned into sobs. He took her into his arms and cradled her. She looked up into his face as she reached for a tissue nearby. "I know it's not fair because once I knew I was pregnant I said for you to go ahead and call Sam. I should have had more faith that God would have provided another way."

"Another way? No. That was the only way. I wouldn't want another way. To me, Sam's offer was a gift from God. He showed me I didn't have to stop being a Jew."

"Daniel, no one ever asked you to do that."

"When we were at the wall in Jerusalem when I received that note, God pierced my heart. But since then, there doesn't seem a way ... a sincere way I can express the devotion I should have toward Him." Taking her hands into his, he explained, "Reciting the *Shema* is the only way I have to try to worship Him. When it is on my lips, I am a Jew, Naomi. Yes, I know Yeshua is our Messiah, but I'm still a Jew." He let go of her hands and reached for a tissue. "I'm doing the best I can."

"It was different for me. I needed to know I could be forgiven. So, for me His suffering on that cross was personal—he died for my sins—I needed to be forgiven." She pursed her lips, knowing she was about to open the door to a subject she had wanted to talk about for a long time. "But you've … well, been so good all your life."

"Look, I'm not all emotional like you. I know that."

"I don't think of it as emotions, but for me, it was an experience—an undeniable one. Yeshua just broke into my life—and He overshadowed all my fears, my shame, wounds that had been crippling me. When I experienced His love, suddenly I was like a ballerina. Like I was gliding and not walking. So I guess I don't worry how to worship Him. I want my love to burst forth just like His did for me. If I lose knowing Him and His presence—the air becomes empty. There's nothing in it. Empty air. Wasted air. But with His presence, glistening honey plumps up every molecule in the air. Daniel, I don't want to go back to a one-dimensional delusion of reality—reality is His presence."

Too many words—he told me he can't follow when I go on and on.

Naomi took a breath. She needed to stop with her too-many-words, but include Daniel. "The day in Brooklyn when I met you in front of the synagogue, I was looking for how to find forgiveness, but Judaism never answered me. Only Jesus did. And with Sam making you take away the cross, it's like taking my joy, my peace. … My sweet husband, my relationship with God is through that cross." She paused and reached for another tissue, but the box was empty.

"Here, I only used half of mine."

She accepted his offer and with the second-hand tissue she dried her eyes while together they shared a laugh. She then told him, "I guess it's different for me than for you. You've been so good all your life. For me, well, I wasn't, so that cross is personal to me."

With her head now resting on his chest and his arms holding her, he admitted, "That's the problem—it has never been personal for me." Naomi, still being held by Daniel, lifted her head to look at him. Brushing a few stray hairs from her forehead, he explained, "That time in Jerusalem, at the Wall—for that short time, yes, it

113

was personal. But then I was thrown into the world of Christianity while I also needed to earn a living for us. I can't explain it, but somehow I think I needed more time in Israel." He gently moved her away and he rose from the chaise lounge. After taking a few steps away, he turned back. "It's like God's work in Israel wasn't finished."

An electric moment transpired between them as their eyes met. Soon both exclaimed, "Yes."

Naomi volunteered, "I'll call and cancel the counseling appointment."

Daniel nodded. "And I'll call the airlines."

Luggage having been hoisted onto the conveyor belt, Daniel checked an overhead monitor to check their gate number. Naomi swiveled her head looking for Zac to come through one of the doors.

"He'll be here, honey. Parking's not easy. Look, he made it on time to drop us off. He's very capable—with all the traffic getting us to the airport. I'm proud of him. Very proud."

"But what about his sister? Tamara was supposed to meet us here, too."

Daniel took hold of Naomi's elbow and edged her to the right. "Here's our boy."

Breathlessly rushing to his parents, Zac called out, "Parking was crazy. Where's Tam? Did she show?"

Both answered, "Not yet."

Daniel held up their boarding passes. "But we're all set, and we've got time til we have to get to the gate."

Zac took out his phone and offered, "I'll call her."

Naomi asked, "Can I use your phone and call her?" Once it was placed in the palm of her hand, she stared at it, brows furrowed.

She saw Tamara using something like this—matter of fact, she was on it all the time, but Naomi never understood how it worked.

Zac chuckled and reached out his hand. "Here. I'll call her. But you guys need to get a phone like this so you can call once you're in Israel. And how long before you get back? You never said."

Daniel turned to Naomi, shrugged his right shoulder, and smiled. "That's because we're not sure yet."

Naomi added, "We bought only one-way—"

"What? Are you—?"

Daniel straightened the collar of Zac's denim jacket. "Relax, we'll be back."

"Your father and I just need—." Naomi's eyes shifted as she exclaimed, "There's Tam."

After running towards each other, Tamara exclaimed, "I was so afraid I was going to miss you. *Bubbe* needed me to help change her sheets."

"Oh, honey, how is my Mom? I feel so selfish leaving her while in the middle of her treatment."

"Mom, listen, she told me to tell you she was happy for you. It's been her dream, she told me, to go to Israel. And she's so happy you get to go for your second time." Tamara grimaced and tilted her head. "I hope you don't mind, I told her you'd take her next time."

"Will there be a next for her? How is she? The radiation now that she's agreed to do it, is it taking much out of her?"

"She's doing great, Mom. Aharon has been right there for her."

Daniel and Naomi looked at each other with startled eyes and in chorus asked, "Aharon?"

Tamara cut her eyes over to her brother for a brief moment. He smiled, turned to their parents, extended an arm showing an open palm directed toward their parents. He then mouthed, "Tell them."

"Okay, here we go. Aharon is Dr. Abadi's first name. Kinda like Aaron, but with an 'h'."

Seeing his cheek twitching, Naomi tried to intervene. "Daniel—"

Daniel coughed into his fist, and then declared, "He's Muslim, Tamara."

"No, he's not Dad. He's a Christian—oh, but I forgot you're not a Christian, are you? So, like, what are we, Dad? Mom?"

Zac quickly jumped in. "Hey, don't you have to get to your gate—it looks like the line might be kinda long."

Chapter Fourteen

He Who Began a Good Work Will Perfect It

How could Daniel sleep in these seats? The large man next to him extended well beyond the armrest, and being in the last row, their seatbacks couldn't recline. Daniel could sleep through a hurricane. With last-minute tickets, there was no picking seats, so here they were stuck between two strangers in the center section. Yet here he slept, as peaceful as if they were at home in their king-sized bed.

She eyed her husband again remembering the last and only time they had flown to Israel. Back then, for the entire flight Daniel would not even acknowledge her. Yet hours after landing at the airport, God intervened and made them one flesh again.

Beauty from ashes. First time she read those words was when she was secretly studying the workbook from the women's center. For years she feared God would never forgive her but when God's loving forgiveness embraced her—as painful as Daniel's rejection was—she could never reject Yeshua. And now their marriage has been fully redeemed by Him. Beauty from ashes—no longer ashes, yet not without conflict.

Please, Lord, you say if we are lacking wisdom to ask and you will give us understanding. You know our every thought. Why can't Daniel

*enjoy You? Has he really given his heart to You? You were supposed
to bring us together, but now ... Lord, please complete the work You
began in Daniel.*

Only ten more hours.

Naomi's perception was wrong, for Daniel's tormented soul pre-
vented him from sleeping.

*You told me Your yoke was easy, and Your burden was light. That's
what You told me. You told me You were my Messiah.*

*Yes, I believe You are—but Your yoke has not been easy. The burden
of knowing my people will perish without You, that burden is not light.
When I touched that sacred wall and You reached down to me, that
connection was something I never felt before. At that moment I knew
You Yourself were speaking to me, Daniel Cantor—but where are You
now? Where is the connection?*

*Your yoke is not easy. My wife, she connects with You. Why can't I?
She was ready to give up everything for You. Even our marriage. Do
you want me to give up being Jewish? Don't You care anymore about
the ones You called the apple of Your eye?*

On their first full day in Jerusalem, Daniel was standing on the
men's side of the Western Wall, witnessing a cluster of old men
reciting their Jewish liturgy. They were rocking back and forth,
while schooling young boys to do the same.

Speaking in Yiddish, the elder told the earnest young students,
"The sacrifice of your lips is acceptable to Hashem, without the
sacrifice of bulls we offer the sacrifice of praise. Cry out to the off-
spring of David, that He may hasten to come. We must be zealous
to perform *Tikkun Olam*[6] and He will come to rebuild our temple
and bring the glorious Messianic age. This is why we are here, is it
not? He is coming."

---

6   Repairing the World (social action and the pursuit of social justice)

The students joined by chanting, "He is coming, He is coming. He will rebuild our temple."

The rabbi closed by saying, "Blessed are you, Hashem Hashem."

The students echoed, "Blessed are you, Hashem."

The rabbi admonished the boys, "Now, pick up the yoke of the law. It is your burden and your honor."

Daniel's stomach knotted, recalling how he, too, had been taught to carry the yoke of the law and to admonish others to do so as well. He made his way to the end of the partition which separated him from Naomi, and thankfully she was already there.

Grieving and with a burning desire to flee from this place, he was only further saddened seeing his wife wearing the mandatory skirt which covered her knees and the top that hid her shoulders and upper arms. But she was still Naomi—his Myomi. Even garbed like the many women who were tucking small pieces of paper between the crevices of the stones, she stood out.

Her face lit up for a moment upon seeing Daniel, until she saw his tears. He hooked elbows with Naomi and said, "We don't belong here. We have to go." He guided them to a coffee shop on Ben Yehuda Street, where they grabbed a couple of seats and ordered coffee. Naomi fanned away the cigarette smoke that surrounded them.

"Daniel, what is it?"

"How do I . . . ? They are teaching *narishkeit*[7] to these children."

Naomi tapped Daniel's hand as she looked around. "You should keep your voice down."

In a softer voice, he said, "Naomi, where—how—do I reach them? I can't and here are these rabbis acting so pious, trying to please God, but they are lost, and they are taking the youth with them." His voice raised again as tears pooled in his eyes. "I'm a Jew and these are my people. But they are lost. Sam said having a messianic congregation would be effective. Jewish people would

---

7   Jewish slang for foolishness

have their eyes opened to the truth. Sure, right—then why are ninety-five percent of our members Gentiles?"

Naomi looked at Daniel for a long moment as if studying a book. "You're trying too hard, at least I think you are. We were going to walk around the old city, but maybe we could just relax— maybe if you don't work so hard at it, God would speak to you. Maybe we should just go to the beach today."

Was he trying too hard? "You're probably right." But he hadn't come for beaches, he came here to once again connect with God. This wasn't just some frivolous vacation.

Their departure was sharply interrupted as a band of troubadours parted the crowd, singing in Hebrew and playing violins, guitars, an accordion, and a flute. Over and over they sang about Yeshua.

A gray-haired man with a matching beard held up a megaphone and proclaimed in a thick Israeli accent, "Yeshua came to put a finish to religion and made a way that you could come into direct contact with God—the God of Abraham, Isaac, and Jacob. Did you ever think about that? Eh?"

From his backpack, the man retrieved and handed out books to those gathered in the crowd. "Take, this is my story, how God changed me. Take." He came to Daniel and offered his book, which Daniel accepted. Before he could get away, Daniel said, "I need to talk to you. What is your name?"

With a firm handshake, he said, "Ezra." His bright blue eyes sparkled. "And you?"

"I'm Daniel, and this is my wife Naomi."

He kept hold of Daniel's hand as he bent from the waist to hear them better. "Strong names. Visiting?"

Daniel nodded and asked, "Do you know of a messianic congregation we could visit?"

Ezra put his hand on Daniel's shoulder. "Haven't you heard, brother? The veil was torn." He studied Daniel.

"Can I talk to you? Do you have some time that we could speak in private?"

Within an hour, Ezra sat across from Daniel and Naomi at the café they had left. Ezra brimmed with life and his voice crackled with excitement. Yet with all his exuberance, he also listened intently. After hearing Daniel's story, he asked, "So, Rabbi, how many Jewish people are coming to your congregation?"

That was the question, wasn't it? "Not many."

Ezra poured honey into his coffee. "You know what I have found?"

Daniel shook his head but leaned in closer to Ezra.

"Whether it's doing all the messianic prophecies or keeping all the customs to try and prove that we're still Jewish, if you don't reach their heart, it stays like stone." He made a fist and put it over his heart, gently pounding it. He then spread his arms and with palms up, he shrugged. e then "And all this time our Messiah is weeping. He longs to give them a heart of flesh. O Jerusalem, O Jerusalem…" He shook his head as he peered into his coffee. Then tilting his head, he asked, "Do you have children?"

Daniel nodded while Naomi quickly said, "Twins."

"So, Daniel, Naomi, do you ever try to get your children's attention? Maybe warn them, even scold them?

"Of course," Daniel said.

"Give me just one of their names."

Naomi answered, "Tamara" as Daniel said, "Isaac."

"Isaac. Strong name. Tamara, too. Named after Tamar?"

"Yes, how did you know?"

Ezra's eyes twinkled. "Let's put bookmark there, okay? Let's take the name Isaac. So, Daniel, when you want to talk to your son, maybe get his attention—warn him or maybe you're simply sad for him. So, at those times do you ever say his name twice? Eh?" Ezra frowned and slowly rocked his head from side to side, and as if pleading said, "Isaac, Isaac." His playacting stopped as he turned to Daniel, "Yeshua—He cries Jerusalem, Jerusalem."

Daniel gasped and stared at Ezra, who rose from his seat and walked to Daniel. "Please, we meet later—in a couple of hours? Just you and me. A beach? Quiet place to sit, to walk, to talk."

It was a perfect evening. The golden hour at the beach. A brilliant vibrant sunset with the Mediterranean Sea reflecting the colors of paradise.

Ezra allowed the stillness to wash over Daniel, walking silently alongside him, until Daniel turned and asked, "Tell me, Ezra, what do you have against Messianic Judaism?"

Ezra placed his arm on Daniel's shoulder and pointed with his chin to a bench conveniently placed at the shoreline. Once seated, Ezra smiled, his weather-worn skin crinkling around his mouth. "This Messianic Judaism, it divides people. I ask you, brother, how can you divide the Body of Messiah? We are one new man, Daniel. To divide what God joined together, that's a sin, *nu?*"

Daniel looked out at the sea. "I have family I never met. Exterminated. My mother says 'they are no more.' Both my parents carry the scars. I remember as a child my mother every night waking up the whole house because the nightmares made her scream. And my father told me he couldn't stop hearing the man, while a gun was placed on his head, reciting the *Shema*. I don't know why God chose me, to put this responsibility on me. All I know to do is perform the rituals that confirm I am a Jew." He turned to face Ezra. "He made me a Jew. My wife is Jewish, too, but she'd be happy to just join a church, a place where I heard them claim the title 'apple of God's eye' for themselves. When I heard that, it made me sick. God wants me to stay a Jew. He is happy when I worship as a Jew—but one who knows Yeshua is our Messiah. So I choose the messianic way."

Ezra tilted his head, put a finger to his lips. "Rabbi, have you visited the Armenian Quarter here in Jerusalem?"

"No, where is it?"

"In Jerusalem, one of the four quarters in the Old City. What do you know about the Armenian holocaust?"

"What? I never heard about this."

"A quarter of Jerusalem is for Armenians. You see genocide was done to them, too—the Armenians were Christians and the Ottomans wanted to wipe out all the Christians. Some Armenians were nailed to a cross, but still they wouldn't deny Yeshua."

Daniel continued to stare at the ocean. "What do you want me to get from this? So, you are telling me our people don't count—we are just millions of millions of victims. So I should—what?"

"Preach the Gospel—we *ALL* have fallen short of God's glory. The sin of man—*ALL* men, Jew, Gentile, from every tribe and nation. Eh? Only through the blood of the Lamb can we please God. Your Messianic Judaism, does it teach that?"

Daniel rose from the bench and walked toward the ocean. "I do what I think will draw Jewish people, yet all that come to our services are Gentiles! If truth has been revealed to me, I should—I must—reach our own people."

Ezra walked to where Daniel stood and took off his sandals. "I love the sea washing my feet. I went to America—New Jersey—years ago, and missed my sand, my saltwater, couldn't wait to come home."

Daniel held onto Ezra's arm to steady himself as he lifted one foot and then the other, removing his loafers. "I know it's a cliché, but Israel feels like home to me as well."

"Deep calls to deep. God set Jerusalem 'in the midst of the nations and countries that are round about her.'⁸" —Yerushalayim—Jerusalem of Gold. If you look at a globe, there she is, right at the center."

---

8   Ezekiel 5:5

As a young couple moved in their direction, Ezra waved his hand to indicate they should move further along the shoreline. As the two barefooted men walked, Ezra confided, "Something I wanted to say to you tonight, the pain you feel because of our people's rejection of their Messiah, it's Yeshua's pain you are feeling. He has allowed you to experience His anguish." He stopped and turned to face Daniel. "When He came to live inside you, He placed that burden in your heart. It's what made Paul write 'I could wish that myself were accursed from Christ for my brethren, my kinsmen.'"[9]

Daniel dropped the loafers he had been carrying. "Then tell me, please, how do I reach them? If Yeshua put this burden in my heart, then I must be a horrible disappointment to Him. I thought I was doing what He wanted when my congregation began to grow. We celebrate the Feasts every year, we build a sukkah, and at our last Seder we had so many sign up, we had to cater a banquet hall. But within the last year, I had to face the fact that no one joining was a Jew."

"What came first, the chicken or the egg?"

"I speak honestly with you, and you ask me that?" Daniel turned to walk away.

Ezra quickly picked up Daniel's loafers that now lay in the sand and caught up with him. "You forgot your loafers. Will you please let me explain?"

Daniel put his hands out, took his loafers, and shrugged. "I don't know what came first—do you?"

"Rabbi, let me start over. God had no beginning, right? He has always been. Abram, then Abraham, he came later, right?" Once Ezra saw Daniel nod in agreement, he continued. "So, one day, for us Jews there's a beginning, Abram becomes Abraham—God chooses a people. We call ourselves the chosen people, eh? So, *nu,* what were we chosen for? Our Great God, our Creator, we were created to love Him, to worship Him. So, without Him, we invent things to worship."

---

9   Romans 9:3

Ezra rubbed his chin, smiled, and asked, "So how do we reach our people? The same as we reach all people. We must reach their hearts. Blessing the challah, saying kiddush over the wine, blowing the shofar, all the rituals, none of that comes close to reaching their hearts. And what about showing all the messianic prophecies? Will that cause them to bow their knee in repentance? And, most importantly, if you leave out the cross, then there's no need for repentance."

"Leave out the cross—did my wife talk to you?"

"Oh, so she ... I see," he chuckled. "No, Rabbi, she didn't, but let me tell you about something. Years and years ago, I was meeting with a Jewish woman. She let me show her all the messianic prophecies, and I convinced her I was still Jewish, showed her how I celebrated the holidays, all the things we think we need to do. Daniel, do you know what she told me? She said, 'okay already, I get it. He's the Messiah—but so what?' You hear that, Daniel—she asked 'so what?' Ever since that time, I've known why we are to preach Christ and Him crucified. The Gospel, Daniel, the Gospel. If anyone—Jew, the same as with Gentile, if the Holy Spirit doesn't convict you of sin, if your heart is not pierced to know God Himself came and died to pay for your sins, knowing that no good work, no lighting candles on Shabbat, no kiddush, no reciting the Shema, all the rituals, then the heart hasn't been reached. Only knowing the Lamb of God sacrificed Himself for you, making it personal, seeing the sin in your own heart, that's when a heart is reached." Studying Daniel's reaction, Ezra asked, "My brother, have you ever confessed that your righteousness will never fulfill God's law and thanked Yeshua for what He did for you? Have you let Him into your heart?"

Daniel, head downcast staring at the sand, shook his head, and then looked up and asked, "What must I do?"

Upon Daniel's return to their hotel room, Naomi discovered that her prayer had been answered. She knew the moment he opened the door.

Epilogue

astor Ling stood before all those gathered for this special event. "We welcome all of you here today as we have gathered together in the presence of God and these witnesses to join Zac and Elizabeth, and Aharon and Tamara in holy matrimony. Marriage is a gift from God, given to us so that we might experience the joys of unconditional love with a lifelong partner. God designed marriage to be an intimate relationship between a man and a woman. Zac and Elizabeth, and Aharon and Tamara, because your deep love for each other comes from God above, this is a sacred moment, and it is with great reverence that I now ask you to declare your intent." Led by the Pastor, both couples spoke their commitments to their chosen partners, and rings were placed on each new bride and groom.

Pastor Ling guided the couples to face the witnesses as he pronounced, "It is my great honor to introduce to you for the very first time, Mr. and Mrs. Cantor and Doctor and Mrs. Abadi.

Church of all Nations had decorated the fellowship hall beautifully, and Naomi's friend Melinda graciously had chosen to provide the catering, as well as the decorations, and even engaged a sought-after wedding photographer.

Naomi, holding tightly to her mother's hand said, "Let's go meet your new family, Mom."

"So beautiful. Look at your little girl, so beautiful."

Epilogue

In seeing both her Mom and *Bubbe*, Tamara ran to them—as dignified as one can with a long gown and a difficult to maneuver train (especially when you consider yourself a major klutz).

After *Bubbe* stopped *kevelling*[10] over Tamara's exquisite wedding dress, she told Naomi, "If it wasn't for your new son-in-law, I wouldn't be here today. So sweet and gentle. Thank God, knock on wood. If only your father were here."

"Mom, let's go join Daniel at our table."

"Darling, first I want to ask you something?"

Hearing the almost shy sound to her mother's request, Naomi immediately agreed, and together they walked to a private corner at the large fellowship hall. "Mom, what?"

"Your husband, sweetheart. Since you got back from Israel two weeks ago, he seems so different. So much happier—and he doesn't seem to care that little Tammy or Zac aren't marrying someone who is Jewish. It just always seemed to me that being Jewish mattered more to him than anything else."

"Something happened to him in Israel, Mom."

"You know I asked him myself earlier. I don't know how I had the nerve, but I asked him if he was okay with both his children not marrying a Jew. He said, 'Mom, we are all one in Messiah.' I can't get that out of my mind. Would you explain that to me?"

10 To feel delighted and proud to the point of tears. rejoice. exult. glory. delight.

Post-Epilogue

Before the wedding reception ended, Tamara told Naomi, "Mom, I found out who Tamar is. So cool I'm named after her. I can't wait to tell you about her."

Contacting Miriam Finesilver

On Facebook: MichaelandMimi Finesilver (https://www.face-book.com/ELOutreach)

Blog: https://miriamfinesilver.net

Amazon Author Page:
https://www.amazon.com/Miriam-Finesilver/e/B00WT2QGNC

www.ingramcontent.com/pod-product-compliance
Lightning Source LLC
Chambersburg PA
CBHW022136080426
42734CB00006B/391